TANGERINE
TANGO

TANGERINE TANGO

WOMEN WRITERS
SHARE SLICES OF LIFE

Donna K. Barry
Judy Ackley Brown
Stacey E. Caron
Barbara Chapman
Gabi Coatsworth
Dawn Quyle Landau
Chris Rosen
Leah R. Singer
Madeline G. Taylor
Patti Winker
Lisa K. Winkler
Barbara Younger

edited by
LISA K. WINKLER

Tending: A Daughter's Tale • *Football Saturdays* • *You Had a Good Run, Grandma* • *When I Lied About My Age* • *The Sea As Smooth As Glass* © Donna K. Barry| *Serene Green* © Judy Ackley Brown | *Make Way for Dorothy: My Grandmother's Chopped Liver* • *Tart From Seville* • *Food = Love* © Stacey E. Caron | *No Necklace. Period* • *Chasing Chicken Cutlets: Breast Cancer & Me* • *Last Goodbyes* © Barbara Chapman | *The Cabinet* • *Ice Cream Odyssey* • *To My Sister* • *Shrimping* © Gabi Coatsworth | *Ode to Girl, Interrupted* • *Passing Ghost* © Dawn Quyle Landau | *The Flapper* • *Up, Up and Away* • *My Son, The Rocker* © Chris Rosen | *Strangers, Salespeople & Sleeping Beauty* • *A Weighty Issue* • *Saying "I Do" to an Interfaith Wedding* © Leah R. Singer | *Duress? Distress? Dial!* © Madeline G. Taylor | *Santa in a Hurry: Christmas 1960* • *Sweetie's Fudge Shoppe: Not So Sweet!* • *Clotheslines* • *Before Helmets* © Patti Winker | *An Ache? A Break? A Cut? ... Call Dr. Dad* • *Help Wanted: Graduates With Tools!* • *Fashion Advice From Our Mothers* • *Screaming Ice Creams! Dirty Diaper, Garlic & Blue Cheese!* • *Balancing Beliefs: From Yiddishkeit to Orthodoxy* • *No Help Needed: A Mother's Chagrin* © Lisa K. Winkler | *Bless All Buttons* • *Bringing Back Dad* • *Socks* • *Pondering Good and Evil* • *Ditch the Old Model?* • *Valentine's Day 1965* © Barbara Younger

Book design by Solveig Marina Bang

Typeset in Adobe Caslon Pro

A NOTE ON THE TYPE
The Caslon typefaces were designed by
William Caslon (1692–1766) in England.
A Caslon font was used for the first printed version of
the United States Declaration of Independence.

The headline type is St Marie by Stereotypes.
www.stereotypes.de

To
Naomi, David & Madeline

CONTENTS

CONTENTS

Welcome to
Tangerine Tango

BY
LISA K. WINKLER

WELCOME TO *Tangerine Tango: Women Writers Share Slices of Life*.

After publishing my first book, *On the Trail of the Ancestors: A Black Cowboy's Ride Across America*, people asked me what my next book was about. I didn't have one! Though I was looking for ideas. When I hit my one-year anniversary for my blog, Cyclingrandma, I thought it would be fun to put my favorite posts into a book. So I invited several writers, mostly other bloggers I've befriended through blogging, to join the project. Along the way, a couple other writers contributed too.

Why *Tangerine Tango*? I love the alliteration and love the color orange. When Pantone, the Carlstadt, New Jersey-based design company declared 'Tangerine Tango' its 2012 color of the year, I wrote a post about all my orange-toned sweaters and accessories.

I wrote: "Sounds more like a cocktail than a clothing color." I had purchased some colorful key chains created by the Israeli designer, Orna Lalo, and also some of her whimsical jewelry and candlesticks while traveling in Israel, and love how she designs with bright colors and funky shapes. I've never been the basic beige sort, and love the use of color, whether on walls, in towels, or clothes. Lalo writes on her website, "Color for me is a language that has a sound, a smell, a touch and taste."

Without giving the writers any themes, I received submissions that span the entire citrus spectrum, from sour to sweet. Enjoy these colorful slices of life: some sad, some nostalgic, and some humorous, about parents and parenting, childhood, food, farewells, jobs and journeys. Empathize, reminisce, and smile.

An Ache? A Break?
A Cut?... Call Dr. Dad

BY
LISA K. WINKLER

WHEN MY SISTER AND I don't feel well, who do we call? After each other, we check in with Dad.

"Did you call Daddy?" my sister Madeline will say if I call to complain about a particular ailment, anything ranging from an arthritic ache to a zealous zit.

Our father isn't a doctor. But he acts like one. He'll "prescribe" ointments and pills and often supply them for us.

He'll scrounge among the apothecary that has pervaded what once was their bathroom. In place of a traditional medicine cabinet is one closet with three deep shelves crammed with prescription and over-the-counter remedies, some dating back at least 30 years.

At each end of the tile counter, my parents have their own "stash" of drugs. And my father, who uses a plastic shopping bag for his traveling toilet kit, has several of these tucked under the counter. To remind him of each drug's use, long after the prescription label has faded, he writes a key word—"feet", "eyes", for example—on the cap or box. Often these words are written in Yiddish, making it even more difficult for us to find something he suggests we use.

We jest about their drug habits, the gargantuan containers of Advil, and the outdated medications. We tell them they can't take each other's meds when one of their prescriptions runs out. But hey, they're 82 and 84; it works for them.

And my parents aren't alone in finagling how they take pills.

"Nearly three in four Americans do not follow

doctor's orders for taking prescription drugs … One in three patients never even fills the prescription."*

FICO, a credit score company, has developed a medication adherence score to predict who might not take medications as prescribed. They suggest that doctors and insurance companies telephone these people once identified. Not taking proper dosages, skipping dosages, taking pills at the wrong time, combining pills, and so on, can result in unnecessary deaths.

I know I'm guilty of the same behavior. Once I feel a bit better, why bother taking more pills?

The use of multivitamins is also under scrutiny. Lightly regulated, they have no standard formula, and may not be necessary. Healthy eating, many believe, negates the need for multivitamins.

Funny, that's what my mother always said.

* Tara Parker-Pope, 'Keeping Score on How You Take Your Medicine', *The New York Times*, June 20, 2011

Bless All Buttons

BY
BARBARA YOUNGER

What life has this button seen?
A wedding, a funeral,
A cheerful greeting,
A bitter quarrel,
And ordinary moments
Filled with the extraordinary.
Breath and sight,
Words and step,
Taste and touch.
Bless all buttons,
And fasten me to this life
With energy and love.

No Necklace. Period.

BY
BARBARA CHAPMAN

G ROWING UP IN THE 1950S AND 1960S provided my generation with a curious group of customs that our parents introduced to us. We hid under the desks at school during air-raid drills; we were tossed into the back of the family station wagon without seat belts; we inhaled our parents' cigarette smoke; and we didn't wear bike helmets.

But one of the most bizarre lessons imparted to us by adults was how we learned about menstruation.

When I was in 5th grade, all the girls were ushered into the only soundproof classroom in the school. We were greeted by the school nurse, the girls' gym teacher (both female) and a handful of mothers who wanted to share in this event. The school nurse announced to us that we were about to enter a very special time of our lives and that getting your period for the first time was nothing to be ashamed of. (Why then were the windows covered in black construction paper?)

We viewed a Disney film about menstruation; it starred Jiminy Cricket. I always thought Jiminy was male. If he could be in a movie about menstruation, why weren't the 5th-grade boys or any male teachers allowed in the room?

I don't really remember what Jiminy Cricket did in the movie. I doubt he danced around singing, "I'm no fool, no siree... and I won't have a period, I guarantee. Better the cramps for you, not me... for I'm no fool."

After the movie ended and the lights came on, the nurse actually asked us girls if any of us had already started their periods. There were a couple mothers who coaxed their fertile daughters into standing in front of the entire class of 5th-grade girls. And we clapped for them!

Then each girl received a booklet that gave us the "whole" story complete with an illustration of a cross-section of the uterus and instructions on how to keep healthy when you were menstruating. For sure, having a period was nothing to be ashamed of, but we had best not swim, nor ride a bike. We needed extra sleep. We would want to shower more frequently and use some sort of powder on our sanitary napkins to prevent odor.

Yet there was nothing to be ashamed about.

The boys huddled on the playground as we were dismissed from this informative event. With booklets in hand, the "bad girls" huddled with the boys, sharing this 5th-grade pornography. Some of them actually sold their books to some of the boys.

The sanitary napkin deemed appropriate for girls our age was about the size of a twin mattress, and it had two long tails, one on each end, that had to be wound around little prongs on the sanitary belt. Only grown women (preferably married women) used tampons.

Many years later, I gave birth to a boy and then

a girl. When Lynn was born in 1984, she was the first girl in the family in 17 years. A few days after her birth, I purchased a very sweet pendant, rather abstract, depicting a seated woman leaning in, coddling her baby. The pendant was not even three quarters of an inch in diameter. Sterling silver with a light silver chain. Very tasteful, simple, and lovely. Every time I looked at it, it reminded me of my beautiful little girl and how much I cherished her.

I planned to give it to my daughter on the day of her first period. We would go to lunch, hold hands and relish the joys of being part of the whole rhythm of life: the sun, the earth, the cycles of the moon. I'd also give her my copy of *Our Bodies, Ourselves* that I had purchased in college. I wanted her experience to be so much better than mine.

New Year's Day, 1997. Lynn wakes up grumpy. She has a skiing date and she can't find her lift pass. She can't find her ski boots. And, she tells me, "Mom, I got my period."

Oh my. The clouds parted, a beautiful beam of sunlight entered through her bedroom window and, if you listened closely, you could almost hear the soft lilting voice of Joni Mitchell singing "The

Circle Game" ("and the seasons, they go round and round and the painted ponies go up and down, we're caught on a carousel of time ..."

"Oh, my baby! Congratulations! How do you feel? Do you have cramps? Would you like to have some hot tea? Shall we go out for lunch? You can always go skiing another time. I'm sure you don't want to be on the slopes anyway. Oh, I almost forgot. Come in my bedroom."

'Mom! You are making way too much of this!'

I opened my closet door and reached to the high shelf to retrieve a box of maxi pads, the book, and the necklace, wrapped in a pretty little box.

"*Mom*! You are making *way* too much of this! You are embarrassing me. And I don't have time to read this hippie book, and I have my own tampons, thank you."

I am crushed. Why was this so important to me? And why was it so unimportant to my daughter?

"Tampons? You have tampons? My God, Katie. Will you at least open the present?"

"Okay, okay. It's very pretty. Thanks. Could you

put it in my jewelry box for me? I don't want to wear it skiing. I might lose it."

"So, you still want to go skiing?"

"Yeah, Mom. I'm not dying. I have my period. Big deal. You need to chill, Mom."

I put away the gifts, helped Lynn find her ski pass and boots, and bid her a fond farewell as she headed to Powder Ridge.

SEVERAL YEARS LATER, our Basset Hound, Mabel, came trotting into the kitchen while the kids were having breakfast, leaving a bloody trail behind her. Alarmed, I picked her up and checked her, fearing she had hurt herself. She had gone into heat for the first time. I gathered her 40 pounds into my arms. "Oh. Mabel! My baby! You're a woman now! I'm so proud of you."

Lynn shoveled a spoonful of granola into her mouth and said, "Hey Mabel, I have a necklace for you."

Ode to Girl, Interrupted

BY
DAWN QUYLE LANDAU

K IDS ARE WIRED to grow up and shake the tree, right? So when our daughter threw us a curve ball, it was bound to be something truly noteworthy. It was; and it all comes back to Israel. Yep, that tiny country that everyone seems to fight about is where my girl got interrupted. It's where our solid relationship took a hard right. First, she went on a two-week trip with Birthright*, the winter of her freshman year at college. There,

* An educational organization that sponsors trips to Israel for young adults

she fell in love with an Israeli man. She returned the following summer and fell in love with the country, and then she fell deeply in love with her faith. Our daughter told us that she was going to study in Israel her junior year, and she came home deeply immersed in a faith that we barely recognize as our own.

My husband is Jewish, and we've raised all three kids in the Jewish faith, but our faith is the reformed brand. The watered down, less strict, simpler brand of Judaism, which (I admit) does what's easiest, while still remaining Jewish. We raised our kids in a Jewish faith with years of Sunday school, Bar and Bat Mitzvahs and attendance on the High Holy Days. Our faith leaves room for bacon, Dungeness Crab, driving on Fridays and Saturdays, using light switches, and calling ourselves Jews even though we do all of those things.

Our daughter has gone a different route on the road to Jerusalem. She has embraced a very conservative Judaism, that we do not share nor entirely understand.

Intellectually, we get most of the edicts that she now follows, even if we don't like them. We have accepted that she will leave our house Friday night and return Saturday, staying with her Chabad Rabbi and his family. We know she is safe and loved, but we don't see her most weekends. We accept that she will no longer eat the meals I prepare, as none of my dishes, pots or pans, let alone oven and stove, are kosher. She cooks on a small two-burner stove that sits at the end of the kitchen island reminding me daily that I can no longer feed my girl.

> My girl ... was gone and a new girl was in her place

When all of this started, that cooktop chastised me daily. It seemed to sit there and yell: "You're not her Mom anymore! You can't feed her like me, you don't understand her like me; she needs me! You're all washed up! But wait, don't wash her dishes. They're kosher, you're not." Yes, that stupid cooktop called me out daily.

I tripped over her kosher dishes, I got all tied up in knots each time I planned dinner, wondering if maybe I could make one little thing she liked, and pull her back into the fold. I baked the gluten-free things she liked, only to remember, again, that my pans were not kosher. My oven wasn't kosher. I wasn't Jewish, let alone kosher.

Before you start thinking that my whole relationship with my girl ended up being about food and cooking, it was much bigger than that. While I had never converted, I changed my whole life to raise my kids as Jews. Foolishly, in my youthful mind, I thought I had to toss aside all of my previous traditions and rituals, to show my family that I was raising Jewish children. No more big family Christmases. I never brought my kids back to see family at the holidays, and my husband's family has never entered my home at Christmas time or seen our Christmas tree. I clung to that one ritual, and still do. No Easter baskets that had made my childhood so colorful and exciting. No bunnies or fancy clothes each spring. I had embraced all of the things that I thought were (reformed) Jewish, much of it revolving around cooking and family-centered holidays. I wanted to be a true Jewish mother, without formally converting. I spent 21 years thinking I'd succeeded. My three kids were Jews, despite my background.

So when my daughter went to Israel and found out that she wasn't really Jewish in Israeli eyes, our whole life and our relationship turned upside down. She came home from Israel and said that she couldn't eat my food anymore; that she would leave our house each weekend. She started dressing more conservatively; she began praying several times each day and refused to go to restaurants with us. She didn't attend a good friend's Bar Mitzvah because it was too far to walk, and it was the Sabbath. It was the curve ball of all curve balls, and I never saw it coming. It hit me right in the face!

The girl who I had always been so close to was suddenly a young woman I could barely speak to. We argued most of the summer. I felt an urgent need to turn her around, get her back, convince her that she was going the wrong way. She was set on showing me that this was her life. That seems an obvious thing, until you're facing it. All summer, still fighting this change, I threw up questions and challenges at every turn. I felt rejected and hurt. I felt like I'd done everything I could to be a Jewish mother, and now I wasn't that at all.

The fact that her 100 percent Jewish father wasn't

Jewish enough either, didn't really register as much. The fact that everything we do as a Jewish family, wasn't Jewish enough and that this was impacting grandparents, aunts, uncles, cousins, friends of the family, her friends, registered, but was merely a blip on my screen. What burned the most was that my girl—the girl who told me everything, the girl who seemed to think everything I did was great—was gone, and a new girl was here in her place.

A good friend has pointed out several times: "Aren't you glad she's absorbed in something she really believes in, that she's passionate about, versus some vapid endeavor?"

Yes, I am; but it's still painful to see her headed in the opposite direction from us. I felt like I was thrashing in deep, choppy water, for months.

We've moved through it. I've gradually learned to sneer back at the cooktop and, sometimes, when my daughter is not around, I give it the finger. I don't let it call me out anymore; I do the calling. I demand that it be kept clean and tidy. I give it the respect it's due, because I love my girl, but no more.

I don't try to think of meals I can make; there

aren't any. I don't try to convince her that it's hot out and long (modest) sleeves and long pants are foolish, that my spare ribs are still amazing, that lobster once a year is glorious, or that taping the light switch in the fridge off, for Shabbat, is odd. I have accepted that I can't reach her from Friday at sunset until Saturday at sunset, no matter what the urgency. When her grandmother died, I wanted so much to have my daughter there, as we washed her body and said goodbye, but it was Shabbat, and I had to let that go too. I told her Grammy was gone, a few hours later, when she walked to synagogue for a Bat Mitzvah. These are things she lives by now, whether we accept them or not.

When her grandmother died, I wanted so much to have my daughter there, but it was Shabbat

My girl and I got interrupted, right in the middle of what has been a 21-year love affair. We got interrupted right when I most wanted to share her adventures and see where she'd go. I wanted to hear about the dates she'd have, the classes she'd take, the parties she'd go to. While some of that is still possible, much of it has been lost this year, in wrapping my head around this new woman who lives a very different life than mine. I have had to pull back the reins on my injured heart and try to find a new rhythm to enjoy with her. I have struggled against it for much of the process, and only recently started to accept our new "normal."

I know my daughter will find her own path, whether it's the one she's on right now, or another that she hasn't seen yet. I know that I will do whatever it takes to for us to work our way back to the groove we once had.

Obstacles may remain, but we'll figure it out.

Years ago, my family wasn't happy with my choices. There is obvious irony in the fact that I fought to marry a Jewish guy, whose family did not approve of a non-Jewish girl, while my own daughter is fighting to be more Jewish. Karma, man, it sucks sometimes.

Make Way for Dorothy: My Grandmother's Chopped Liver

BY
STACEY E. CARON

I LOVE CHOPPED LIVER. This is a love-hate thing for most people. I have tried making it Mario Batali's way, with red wine, anchovies and vinegar, and Ina Garten's way with Madeira and shallots (too fancy for me), and though they are both excellent spread on a crostini topped with frizzled onions, I will stick to my roots and make my grandmother's chopped liver. To me it is always the best.

My grandmother served it as a first course during Jewish holidays on a bed of iceberg lettuce and served it with an ice cream scoop. She had an old-fashioned meat grinder that she used to grind the calves' liver after broiling. Her chopped liver was better than anyone else's.

As she got older, she started making chopped liver with chicken livers because it was just easier than bringing the grinder up from the basement. She has been gone for a few years now, and I am so glad she wrote down all of her recipes for me. I like to continue the traditions. I make this delicacy for Passover only, and it brings back a lot of good memories. Move over Ina and Mario, here comes Dorothy!

GRANDMA DOROTHY'S CHOPPED LIVER

1 *lb* chicken livers, washed
and membranes trimmed
2 large yellow onions, thinly sliced
Schmaltz (chicken fat) or vegetable oil
(use the schmaltz if you can!)
3 hard-boiled eggs
Lots of salt and pepper

In a large, heavy skillet, fry onions in chicken fat (or vegetable oil) on medium heat for about 7 minutes until golden. Salt chicken livers and add to same pan with the onions. Simmer for about 15 minutes until all the pink is out of the liver. The onions will continue to cook down. In a small bowl, mash hardboiled eggs with a potato masher and set aside. When livers are done, with a slotted spoon, transfer them to a food processor. Leave onions in the pan. Pulse once or twice, leaving the livers chunky. You *do not* want a puree. Add liver and onions to a large mixing bowl and mix together, getting up all the onion bits and oil left in the frying pan. If it looks too dry, add a tablespoon of vegetable oil. Now add chopped egg, and salt and pepper to taste. Garnish with parsley or thyme. Great on matzoh, and iceberg lettuce!

Enough for 8 people.
Double it if you have a crowd.

The Cabinet

BY
GABI COATSWORTH

I T WAS TIME TO TACKLE THE GARAGE. I'd been meaning to do it for some time, ever since we'd finished painting the new house, in fact. I looked around and wondered where to start.

I sighed as my eyes came to rest on the small mahogany cabinet. It was at the back of the garage, leaning rakishly to one side. The shelves that should have been inside were stacked next to it, probably preventing its complete collapse. I considered what to do with it. The cabinet had been stored in the garage ever since we'd moved from our big house into a cottage and I still hadn't managed to find a spot for it in our tiny new home.

I picked my way across the garage, trying to avoid tripping over the assortment of objects that had been deposited there "just for now" over the last few months. I reached the cabinet, and checked it from several angles to see whether it looked any better close up. One of the doors was hanging open, and the thin stripe of walnut inlay was covered with a layer of builder's dust. I ran a finger over the top of the cabinet, drawing a heart, then an arrow, then my and Jay's initials.

I wondered whether to take the cabinet to the furniture repair man who had refinished it for me 10 years before. I could see him, shaking his head, telling me, his Italian accent lacing his voice, "Gabi, it's not worth fixing this."

I was quite sure my daughter wouldn't want it. She'd grown up seeing the cabinet behind the kitchen door in our London flat. I kept canned and dry goods inside and also the biscuit tin. I remembered the times when she'd sneaked a biscuit, thinking I hadn't known, and smiled.

I brought my thoughts back to the cabinet, as I reached for a dusting cloth and wiped it down, erasing the heart on the top. You must stop being so sentimental, I chided myself. Looked at with dispassionate eyes, what was the cabinet, really? Some mahogany that a Victorian cabinet maker had assembled into a piece of furniture. That was the way to look at it: surplus wood should be taken to the town dump.

There was that man from Jamaica who worked there, I remembered. Whenever I took cardboard containers to be recycled, we would exchange a few words about the weather (not as nice as Jamaica) or the number of reggae stations you could find on the radio (more than in Jamaica). Now there was someone who was always finding things to fix up; maybe he could use the cabinet. He'd put that broken stool together, so he had somewhere to sit while he operated the crusher. I would ask him whether he'd want it.

I had lived with the cabinet for at least 35 years, but had seen it long before, when it stood in my great aunt's house. I'm not sure what else she kept in there but whenever my sisters and I went to her house for afternoon tea, she would open the cabinet door and extract a small tin of Harrogate Toffee. Then she would present one of us with a small, silver toffee hammer. The lucky girl would strike the toffee as hard as possible, and distribute the shattered remains to the rest. I still recall the way that toffee stuck to the roof of my mouth.

My spinster great aunt ... would open the cabinet door and extract a small tin of Harrogate Toffee

When she died, some years later, she left me this little cabinet. I sorely needed furniture, since I had married young and had no money to spare for luxuries. Victorian furniture was in fashion then, and the neat lines of the cabinet appealed to me. I polished its rich mahogany with beeswax, and stored my collection of long-playing records inside; they fit perfectly. A glass vase glinted on top of it. Later, it had been moved to the kitchen and, when I moved to America, the cabinet came too. It had seen service in the dining room, where we rearranged the shelves to hold wine glasses and bottles. Later it migrated to the children's room, where a collection of half-made model planes found their way inside, and untidy piles of school papers drifted across the top. Just before our most recent house move, I found it in the basement, filled with old letters and photographs that I moved into a plastic bin.

I was wasting time. I gripped the top of the cabinet, and braced myself to lift it. As I did so, the top of it came away in my hands and the sides fell apart. I stared at it for a second, before making a small pile of the remains and loading them into the back of my car.

I tried not to look into the rear-view mirror as I headed for the town dump. Driving through the gates, I looked around for my Jamaican friend. He wasn't there. Slowly, I maneuvered the car towards the gaping jaws of the compacting machine. I parked, took out the wooden pieces and walked over to the compactor. I was finding this very difficult. It was like throwing a piece of my history away. I turned away from the compactor and made for the chain link fence nearby. I leaned the mahogany shelves against the fence, and then went back for the rest of it. Revving the engine of the car, I accelerated out of the dump. As I glanced into the rear-view mirror for one last look, I saw the dump attendant at the chain link fence. He was collecting the wood. He would glue it together. Wouldn't he?

Santa in a Hurry: Christmas 1960

BY
PATTI WINKER

W E AWOKE AND RUSHED to the stockings and the tree, only to be stopped by the sight of Dad digging around in the hallway closet. Dad was a big man and this was a small closet, so the sight alone made us laugh.

There was Dad, pulling presents out of the closet saying "Santa must have been in a hurry because he left all the presents in the closet. Here's one for Mary Lee, and one for Annabelle, and this one is for Barbara Jean." And so on.

We were puzzled. What had happened? Santa had never been too busy to leave the presents under the tree.

And, where was Mom?

Santa had brought us another present in the middle of the night. A baby brother. "Santa" was too busy to put the gifts under the tree.

I imagine Mom, having just given birth, trying to figure out how she and Dad were going to pull this off. How would they preserve the magic of Santa and Christmas morning for us kids at home? Mom, in the hospital telling Dad where the gifts were hidden, and Dad coming home and carrying out the mission with seven kids waiting and wondering what was going on.

I don't remember the gifts that year. Maybe it's because we left everything behind when Dad piled us in the car to go see our baby brother, Matthew Jon. We stood at the nursery window with our noses pressed against the window, much like a bakery. We stared at all those little miracles bundled in pink and blue. And then we saw the crib with our name written on the card.

Chasing Chicken Cutlets: Breast Cancer & Me

BY
BARBARA CHAPMAN

I WAS DIAGNOSED with Stage 2 breast cancer in 2001. I found the lump myself. All my previous mammograms had been clean. In two months, I went from having a clean mammogram to having a tumor that was 4.5cm. That was bigger than my boob! My sick right breast was about to graduate me into a full "A" cup, but, it's no fun being a more buxom broad if you are filling your bra with cancer.

I shaved my head in advance of the chemo. My best friend outfitted me with a different hat every time I went for my appointment. Once, I was a Viking warrior, another time, The Cat in the Hat. Once a Martian.

After the chemo came the surgery. I woke up with four drains and lots of bandages. The healing process was quick. My daughter helped me find a prosthetic bra that would hold my fake breasts that looked kind of like two skinless chicken breast cutlets, covered in shrink wrap.

Chemo and surgery behind me and two chicken breast cutlets in front of me, I began radiation: Daily for six weeks. I would dress in a hospital gown and lie on a big table staring up at the ceiling in the breast cancer radiation suite. The staff had posted sexy men in skimpy bathing suits on the ceiling.

One day while undressing to don my hospital gown before radiation, one of my chicken cutlets hit the floor. It bounced. It rolled. It went under the dressing room door and made its way out into the corridor, running away like the Gingerbread Man. I had to suit up and chase my boob.

About five years ago, one of those pesky chicken

cutlet inserts popped out of the top of my bathing suit and is now drifting around somewhere in Long Island Sound. I then decided to consider reconstruction that would use some of my extra belly fat. The surgeon was able to do a "tramflap" where he divided the belly fat in two, reopened the mastectomy scars, and fashioned new breasts from the fat. Nothing foreign in my body; just a lot of fat that has shifted positions. A tummy tuck and a boob job all at once.

During a later surgery, I had my breasts "detailed," with nipples and aureoles, so they'd look more real. Opting to go under the knife again, I gave my surgeon a little surprise. When he opened my gown, he saw written in black magic marker across my chest: "Thanks for the Mammaries".

My hair never grew back, so I never have a bad hair day. I just pop on a wig and find the sweet spot in every day.

Help Wanted: Graduates With Tools!

BY
LISA K. WINKLER

A FEW DAYS AGO the front storm door of my house wouldn't open. The knob turned but the latch remained stuck. I retrieved a screwdriver and removed the screws around the knob on both sides of the door; the latch didn't budge.

I called the installer, a family-owned window and door company in my town. Within an hour, Jeff returned my call and we set a time for him to come over. He tinkered with the latch and brought out tools, taking the knob and handle apart. The plastic cylinder inside was worn out. He needed to order the part and would return the next morning. As he left, he mentioned how he's the handy man for the company. "The other guys have it easy," Jeff said, "they install doors and windows all day. I have to figure out how to fix things."

His comment, like the annoying door latch, stuck with me.

I remember that my grandparents and parents knew how to fix things. My maternal grandfather, Joe, would repair broken pots and dishes. My mother and I often invoke his talents when a saucepan needs a new handle or a cake plate is cracked and chipped. He'd restore the function of these items, if not their original beauty.

My father, a farmer, invented mechanisms to repair machinery. He still does, applying his "make something out of nothing" attitude to fixing tractors and equipment on my brother's golf range. Over the years, I remember him fixing the dishwasher, washing machine and dryer, and my mother's sewing machine.

My mother mended—and still does—clothing

most of us would turn into rags. She saves everything. "You never know when it might be useful," she says. She's the master of using leftovers; a half a cup of coffee and the juice in an empty pickle jar are added to soups and stews. Children of the Depression, they're the original recyclers; little is ever thrown out.

While waiting for Jeff to return the next morning, reading the newspaper and drinking my coffee—and, while I save leftover coffee to drink, I don't use it in cooking—I read an editorial about what today's graduates need to know.

With graduation season upon us, advice to high school and college graduates abounds. High schoolers, entering college, face uncertain futures. Will the economy be that much better in two or four years to improve their job prospects? Reports for college graduates have been equally worrying. Without employment, their ability to pay off student loans becomes compromised.

Jeff arrived and fixed the door. He mentioned he had so much work that the company was hiring another handy man (or woman).

I thought about the editorial and about how

my parents and grandparents could fix things. How they mended, invented, and adapted; how they saved wire bread twists, elastic bands, empty jars, and parts from broken appliances to reuse somewhere else.

I thought about today's graduates. Perhaps our curriculums need to be amended: don't remove what's there, but find ways to add some lessons that give graduates skills that might provide jobs. Like fixing stuck door latches.

Tending:
A Daughter's Tale

BY
DONNA K. BARRY

I PLUNGE MY TROWEL into the moist soil and wrangle out a clump of pansies. These happy yellow-faced flowers are starting to look a little long in the tooth, but still have some life left in them. I can't bear to throw them out, so they'll be getting new life in a pot with other misfit transplants that will be perfect on the shaded patio. This is the happiest time of my day—tending the garden. I would gladly neglect inside chores, work, and even writing, to spend the rest of my summer, and perhaps the rest of my days, tending flowers. I ponder why this is so, but deep down I already know the answer.

From the time I was old enough to walk, I spent my early days following Daddy around the yard. Each summer evening after supper, he'd leave the inside work behind and tend the flowers and garden. Never mind that he'd just spent all day working in someone else's greenhouse—this was the work he loved. We'd putter in the yard together. I'd follow along while he carried buckets of water, sifted composted soil, and scattered pink fertilizer around the stems of young tomato plants. I learned the names of every kind of petunia, marigold and tomato. Big Boy, Early Girl, beefsteak, and cherry tomatoes, all went into the garden behind our greenhouse. Tiny tomato sprigs that Daddy had painstakingly started in our cellar from seeds back in March were now brave little plants that grew into bushes under our care. At the end of our gardening, there would always be time for a wheelbarrow ride, then sitting in Daddy's lap in the cool darkness of the porch until bedtime.

Today, I no longer grow tomatoes, but I have flowers. Perennial gardens of Black-Eyed Susan,

Sedum and Euonymus edge the house and yard, and pots and boxes of colorful annuals brighten the porch and patio. I have never mastered the art of growing geraniums the way Daddy did, but I've learned the art of growing my new favorites. Bright orange Gerbera daisies shade deep blue petunias, and blue lobelia ring delicate maidenhair ferns. Yellow tuberous begonias kiss red verbena in a giant coffee cup, while pairs of Purple Fountain Grass reach for the sky in matching pots. My gardens are more varied than Daddy's were, and just as loved.

Every time I sprinkle handfuls of fertilizer around my plants, and dig into the dark moist soil with my favorite trowel, I remember those days we spent together. Every time I enter a greenhouse and smell the deep, sweet smell of moist earth, I feel the hard-packed dirt of our greenhouse floor beneath my feet, and once again see the rows of tiny seedlings awaiting our care.

Thanks, Daddy, for teaching me to tend.

Ditch the Old Model?

BY
BARBARA YOUNGER

A FEW MONTHS AGO, my husband Cliff said, "I
have something for you to consider."

That line always makes me nervous. And although
the question ended up being a generous one, it did
reach deep into the Oh No What Should I Do?
region of my brain.

"Would you like a new stove?"

Normally, I spring at the chance for something
new. The word "new" suggests small miracles like
more heat or a washing machine that doesn't

dance across the floor. (I live in a 185-year-old house in a small town in North Carolina.) New has its charms!

But a new stove.

Our stove is 60 years old. It came with the house. It has roasted turkeys, sent fudge to a rolling boil, baked birthday cakes, simmered spaghetti sauce, heated hot chocolate and winter wine, and melted Shrinky Dinks.

The stove is down to two burners, one of two ovens, and wouldn't think of self-cleaning. There's a strip of masking tape on the left side of the controls to remind us not to press those switches because, if we do, we might recreate The Christmas Eve Stove Fire of 2004.

But still, the answer to the stove question was "No." Our stove is the Senior Stateswoman of the Kitchen. For now, she stays.

Fashion Advice From Our Mothers

BY
LISA K. WINKLER

I PULLED MY WHITE SKIRT from the closet, thinking I'd better wear it now; I only had a couple more days to do so. My mother always said not to wear white after Labor Day. That got me remembering some of Mom's other fashion advice like "be sure to wear clean underwear and don't use safety pins to fix your bra; sew it!".

I thought how everyone's mother must have done the same thing: volunteering opinions, praise, and criticism. I know I've done my share. I asked about

50 women of all ages and backgrounds to recall what their mothers had said about fashion. Here's a round-up:

On Wearing White

Many contested the idea; declaring how wonderful whites look throughout fall and winter.

"I, of course, strongly remember no white after Labor Day, and not before Easter. That is big in the South."—*Tammi*

"Regarding 'White after Labor Day', as a 'Fashionista', I'll have you know ... that 'rule' *no longer* stands. You can wear white and open-toe heels *all year long*! —*Sakina*

"I write wearing my whites—polo shirt and gray chinos—to set off my summer tan as I take off on a bike ride to see a sailboat on the rocks, skewered by its mast courtesy of [Hurricane] Irene. Can't beat that contrast, tan to white, for the usually pasty set! Signed, 'Always a Sailor'"—*Diana P.*

On Underwear

The appearance and condition of underwear must have kept our mothers awake worrying.

"Make sure your underwear is not only clean, but

not torn. Don't want to wind up in an emergency room with shabby underwear. Don't want to wind up in an emergency room period."—*Mom*

"Mom said 'Make sure you don't have holes in your socks when you go to the doctor.'"—*Adeena*

"Be sure your bra strap doesn't show! Now it's a fashion statement to show your cool, thin, colorful (or not) bra straps!"—*Nancy K.*

"[When I was] growing up in the 60s, my mom was thrilled if I just covered all the 'important' parts and wore a bra." —*Nancy J.*

"Wear a girdle; a jiggly booty is unbecoming. If you have a sheer-ish skirt, a slip is necessary and appropriate."—*Lisa P.*

"My Aunt Elaine always told us: 'Your underwear *must* match. God forbid if you get in an accident and become unconscious, you will be treated better if your underwear matches. The doctors will assume that you have insurance!'"—*Robin*

One friend offered the advice she gives her 20-something daughters: "Always wear something sexy underneath even if no one is going to see it. You will feel fab. Wear a thong, you don't want panty lines."—*Sharon*

On Stockings and Shoes

"Wear pantyhose in the workplace. My mom also made us [wear] only colored tights with short skirts."—*Judy*

"I remember my mom making me change my shoes once on the way to High Holidays. Forget about cleansing and purification, in Northern Virginia the High Holidays were all about fashion. 'Who looks at shoes?' I said, sure that whatever scuffed and inappropriate clodhoppers I had on would meet with God's approval. She looked at me with weary disdain: 'Everybody looks at shoes.'—*Debra G.*

"Fix your shoes. If they are good enough to wear, they should be mended."—*Mom*

"I do remember loving that my mother always bought multiple colors of shoes she liked and always had the bag to match."—*Teri* (My mother had matching gloves, too.)

On Hats and Hair

"You must wear a hat when you go out. Ever hear of a house without a roof?"—*Robin*

"It totally doesn't matter what curlers you put in your hair or where you place them as long as they are curled straight to the head."—*Deanne*

"No straw hats before Memorial Day or after Labor Day."—*Gilla*

"Don't wear a hairstyle you have to keep fixing all day"—*Yaaileith*

On Styles and Patterns

"Mom told me I was too short to wear a bikini when I was 16 and 100 pounds. Now of course, I'm too old and doughy for one."—*Marla*

"My mother was all about wearing anything that was slenderizing: no horizontal stripes, wear dark colors, and she strongly advised against sleeveless blouses."—*Madeline S.*

"My mother liked me to wear one color, or a matching print for both top and bottom and even matching shoes so that I would look taller."—*Beth*

"Never wear yellow because it washes out your skin. I love the color and wear it a lot nowadays. She always told me to make sure my skirts or dresses went below the knee because she thought women's knees were ugly."—*Audrey*

"Short shorts were for your backyard only."—*Betsy A.*

On Being Ladylike

"Leave a little something for their imaginations. A little lipstick never hurt anyone."—*Terri*

"Always get dressed when you go out. You never know who you will run into."—*Judy*

"Your clothes should always be ironed. Clothes must be washed after one use (no re-wearing of clothes, even if you only had them on for church or a few hours)." —*Lisa P.*

"Never wear an all-new outfit. It's ostentatious. Wear something old with something new."—*Betsy*

In General

"The way you dress will be people's first impression of you."—*Nancy P.*

"Sit up straight or you get a hump in your back." —*Pamela*

"The only advice we had from our parents (being in Russia) was to dress warm when it is cold (-40ºC)." —*Yelena*

"Always carry a hanky, and make sure you have 20 cents in case you have to make a phone call." —*Kaye*

On Being Yourself

"What you wear should please *you*. It should not reflect what others think."—*Nita*

I HEAR MYSELF in some of these quotes and know I've commented about cleavage, sheerness, short skirts, tight jeans, no stockings in freezing weather, too-long earrings, and more. I hope my daughter forgives me.

Strangers, Salespeople & Sleeping Beauty
(Thanks a lot, Walt Disney!)

BY
LEAH R. SINGER

ONCE UPON A TIME, there was a mother and a daughter who were at home when they heard a knocking at the door. The dog barked and the little girl ran to the door to see who had come calling.

This isn't a fairy tale. Last week, Sophie and I were home, enjoying each other's company, when I opened the door to a salesperson who was selling financial planning services. Every once in a while, a salesperson will come to our door offering to sell us new windows, pest control, or whole-house painting. All these people say the same thing: "I've been talking to your neighbors and they said blah blah blah …"

So when the financial planning dude said exactly that, I wanted to respond: "Really, you talked to my neighbors? Because every one of you says that same line. So I find it hard to believe that it's true."

You would think if people were going to solicit door-to-door they would get a more creative sales pitch.

The second strange thing about this interaction is the fact that he is selling financial planning services. What kind of person decides to buy financial planning services from a traveling salesperson?! A stranger is the last person I'm going to trust with my financial information. Which leads me wonder if this guy is even a real financial planner.

So finally, after I kicked the salesman off my porch, I decided to use this experience as an opportunity to discuss with Sophie about not talking to strangers. I told her that only Mommy and Daddy can open the door, and we especially do not open the door to strangers. She also should not talk to strangers.

She seemed to understand the concept, relating

to me "that's what the grandmother said to Little Red Riding Hood, and the fairies said to Aurora in *Sleeping Beauty*."

Great, she got it! And then do you know what she said?

"But Mommy, in *Sleeping Beauty*, the Prince was a stranger and Aurora talked to him."

She's right! What do I say to that?

I persuaded Sophie that Aurora really shouldn't have talked to the Prince. I convinced her that the story is make-believe and things that happen in Disney movies don't happen in real life. She understood, she said, but pointed out that it seemed okay to talk to animals. So thanks a lot, Walt Disney, for taking a perfect teachable moment and throwing it back in my face. Evidently, princesses are exempt from the rules of society. Or perhaps the Prince was actually hoping to make a financial planning sale.

Screaming Ice Creams! Dirty Diaper, Garlic and Blue Cheese!

BY
LISA K. WINKLER

DIRTY DIAPER. Unless you're a new parent or a pediatrician, no more description needed. Unless it's an ice cream flavor. It's chocolate with chocolate chunks.

Like sunscreen and bug repellent, watermelon and iced tea, ice cream screams summer. The stands I frequent close shortly after Halloween. They sell pints at half price before unplugging freezers and boarding up windows until spring.

Then grocery store pints and half gallons suffice, occasionally gracing pies à la mode throughout fall and winter.

There's nothing like an ice cream cone. And this summer, there are more flavors than ever to choose from. Creative expression has pervaded ice cream, exposing our palates to culinary experiences akin to dining in ethnic restaurants.

Cheeses—feta, goat's, ricotta or blue—can be found mixed with fruit and vegetables. Savory spices such as paprika, basil, rosemary, curry, pepper and even garlic are offered next to traditional chocolate, vanilla and strawberry. In New Jersey, the Garden State, I've seen "Fresh Corn." For those who skipped breakfast, maple syrup and bacon flavors abound and, for those thinking salad, there's olive oil.

Then there are the flavors, invented by creative vendors, whose names tell the customer nothing. Why don't the stores tape an explanation of these flavors to the front of the case? Instead, customers have to ask what each is, wasting the scooper's time and annoying the impatient Little League team waiting in line.

One stand offers a flavor named for the town's zip code. And "Special Flavor," which changes all the time. Last visit, it was peach. And the imaginative names, like Dirty Diaper, Elephants Never Forget, and Kong.

My visits to the ice cream store are infrequent; I savor every lick. I might ask for a taste of something different and then stick to my usual: coffee or coconut or black raspberry.

As for comfort food, I'll take ice cream. While others might not eat under stress, I'll happily consume the entire kitchen, particularly ice cream.

Years ago, my sister Madeline and I, home from school, took a brand new half-gallon of Heavenly Hash (vanilla and chocolate ice cream filled with white marshmallow swirls, chopped almonds, and dark chocolate chunks) from the freezer. As we vented about our days, gossiping and complaining, we passed the container back and forth, taking a spoonful. And another. And another. Without intending to, we finished the entire carton. We still remember eating that half gallon, an experience we haven't repeated.

Once or twice a summer I'll splurge on a hot fudge sundae with nuts. Homemade hot fudge outshines anything store-bought or even from ice cream stands. Here's my sister's easy recipe. It's divine!

MADELINE'S HOT FUDGE SAUCE

1 can evaporated milk
2 tbsp corn syrup
1/2 cup sugar
2 cups chocolate chips

Mix milk, corn syrup and sugar together in saucepan. Bring to a boil, stirring. Continue stirring on low for 3 to 4 minutes, remove from heat, add 2 cups chocolate chips and stir until smooth. Keeps for weeks in the fridge. Reheat in microwave as needed.

The Flapper

BY
CHRIS ROSEN

Born in 1908, Gertrude Smith was a flapper. Barely 5'2" tall, her blonde hair was neatly combed into a Marcel wave ending just below her ear. She told me once or twice that when she was young she was a "rebel." Her ancestors were Irish coal miners who settled in Scranton, Pennsylvania. She was widowed three times.

Although I wasn't actually raised by my birth mother, I visited her often and eventually, at the age of 11, moved into her home.

I was her last child, and these are some of the things she taught me:

"Signs are for sheep." My mother could always find her way in, around, over or under a problem. She encouraged us to think for ourselves, never to take "No" for an answer, and to always hit back harder when faced with a bully. She did not suffer fools at all. When Nell (my foster mother) and my mother first met as teens, she was sporting a black eye. When asked how she got it, Nell said, "Your mother could swear like a sailor." They didn't know then that both would become my mothers.

'I'll not only walk again. I'll dance on your grave'

"I'll not only walk again, I'll dance on your grave!" After losing her husband to a brain tumor and surviving a near-fatal car accident in that same year—1949—this is what she had to say to her doctors. They told her she would never walk again. The engine of the car had crushed her beautiful dancer's legs—the legs that had won many a late-night dance contest with the Jimmy Dorsey Orchestra. There would be no wheelchair in her future. And there was no relative to care for me, a 10-month-old baby. My grandmother was holding me in the car, and she and my older sister were each in a coma. Nell took me home, and raised me as her own.

"Fine, all the more for the rest of us." This was said whenever I refused to eat something. Nell always took me to visit Mother, and sometimes I'd stay for a weekend. So at times I was an only child, and then I'd have two brothers and a sister. Mother believed in reverse psychology; this was her parental mantra. Surprisingly, it worked. Watching my brothers and sister chow down with glee always made me rethink my decision. Nell made me finish everything on my plate, which I hated. "Waste not, want not" was Nell's motto. With apparent indifference, Mother gave me permission to control my own life.

"You are in your perfect place." A big believer in Norman Vincent Peale and *The Power of Positive Thinking* (this came in her later, post-Freudian years), Mother would hang a picture of something she wanted on the refrigerator. Inevitably, she'd get it. She talked about the science of the mind and eventually became a leader in the Unity Church. I knew she hated most organized religions, so this was puzzling to me. But, in the end, I believe the combination of spirituality and psychiatry brought her a certain peace.

"When they're inside, I'm their mother. When they're outside, they're in God's hands." Having so many children may foster this type of thinking—it is the antithesis of helicopter parenting—more like survival mode parenting. Once, when they were young wives, Nell was having coffee in the dining room with Mother, and saw my older brother Mike teetering on the porch rail, over a 30-foot drop to the back yard. This was her reply, looking serenely at Mike out the bay window, to my nearly panicked foster mother.

You might say I benefited from the Yin and the Yang of motherhood.

Balancing Beliefs: From Yiddishkeit to Orthodoxy

BY
LISA K. WINKLER

THERE'S AN OLD JOKE about Jewish holidays: "They tried to kill us. We survived. Now let's eat!"

That sort of sums up my relationship with Judaism growing up. My family, culturally connected yet spiritually secular, gathered at my grandparents' farmhouse for large dinners: lots of food and lots of people. Grapefruit halves with maraschino cherries, matzo ball soup, roast chicken, and my grandmother's *tayglach*—a dough ball confection hardened with dripping honey and walnuts—and her famous apple strudel, formed the basis of every meal. I remember chasing my cousins around the antique-filled living room, being chided to not break anything and to stay off the furniture, even though it was covered in heavy plastic.

My sister and I were the only Jews in our elementary school until Rochelle Marvin moved to town in 6th grade. We became fast friends; someone else to share the ethnic slurs with—infrequent yet nonetheless hurtful and mean.

My mother insisted we take a day off from school to honor Rosh Hashanah*. Not so much to attend services, but to show others respect for our own religion. People in our community attended church; I joined my friends at an occasional midnight mass or sunrise sermon. Friends expected us to have answers to their questions about Judaism, and assumed we observed its customs and beliefs as they did their religions.

College introduced a new world. I met lots of Jewish kids and many who took it seriously enough to attend services on Friday nights *and* High Holidays. Members of local synagogues invited students for

* Jewish New Year

holiday meals. I attended services, though infrequently; I was with friends, and well-fed.

Still, nothing ever resonated with me spiritually. My husband's college friend, then a rabbinical student, performed our marriage ceremony; my mother, a Justice of the Peace, signed the legal documents. We raised three children with the same sense of Yiddishkeit, an emotional attachment to the culture and identity without the ritual observances. We gave them choices: our eldest opted to do nothing; our second son attended a secular humanistic school; our daughter selected a Reform synagogue to have the Bat Mitzvah her friends were having, complete with a catered party and DJ.

Within two years, both sons became *Baal teshuva*, or the "one who returned," embracing Orthodox Judaism

Then, our second son went to Israel for a year before starting college, participating in Hadassah's year course. Tapped on the shoulder, asked what he was doing for Shabbat, he became intrigued, then hooked. Within two years, both sons became

Baal teshuva, or the "one who returned," embracing Orthodox Judaism. Within a short time, ritual observance became routine: Eating kosher foods, installing mezuzahs on every doorpost, praying three times a day, wearing kippot and tallith and putting on teffilin* and studying tomes upon tomes of Torah text, saying *bruchas* or blessings for everything they eat and drink.

They also began arranged dating, meeting like-minded women through a matchmaker. Both married in 2009. We have three grandchildren.

It's been an interesting journey. Learning and accommodating, doing what I can so they'll eat in my house, respecting beliefs of *all* the children, a tolerance balancing act.

As Jews around the world usher in the new year, and the days of repentance, culminating with the observance of Yom Kippur, the Day of Atonement, I exchange *L'Shana Tova* with other Jews, and wish them an "easy fast." Through reflection, prayer, and penitence for misdeeds, we hope to be inscribed for another year in the "Book of Life."

---

* Mezuzahs: parchment inscribed with verses from the Torah. Kippot: ritual hat. Tallith: prayer scarf. Teffilin: phylacteries, or boxes, containing quotations from Hebrew scripture.

Sometimes, I attend services with my sons and their wives, sitting on the women's side of the shul. I feel a bit left out—I don't know the songs or the prayers. I don't read or speak Hebrew. Yet, I enjoy the sense of community.

I'm a staunch believer in our nation's Bill of Rights. Freedom of religion is paramount. I look at my grandchildren; like my own children, I hope they'll have freedom to choose.

Passing Ghost

BY
DAWN QUYLE LANDAU

*I wrote this in honor of my mother, Carole, who
died December 31, 2011, of Huntington's disease.
She was 68.*

THE SILVER CAR PULLED UP to the light, preparing to turn left and pass me in the opposite direction. The driver caught my eye, and I held my breath. My car made the right at the green arrow on its own, as my head pivoted in slow motion, to look more closely at the driver of the silver car, turning and passing me on my left. Stunned, my senses racing, I watched the woman navigate her turn, while my heart sped.

She looked so much like my mother that I had to force myself to look away and focus on the road ahead. As our cars moved past each other, I looked at her more closely. The resemblance was striking. The tight line of her jaw, the determined look, the way she held the wheel lazily in her hands as she looked around her, as if driving were an afterthought: all of it was my mother. Each nerve in my body tingled, the synapses fired the message *she is gone*, while my heart tugged in disbelief.

Of course, even as it was happening, I was acutely aware that it wasn't, couldn't be, my mother. She had been dead for four months; her ashes sit in a box beside the fine china she loved so much. By the time Huntington's disease finally took her, she relied on a walker and her ability to navigate was gone. She had become a frail woman who could not care for herself. Before her death she hadn't driven a car in nearly five years and I would no more expect to see her behind the wheel than I'd expect to see my 12-year-old niece driving. Yet in that moment, as that silver car drove past me, I wanted desperately to turn around, follow it, and find my mom.

The rest of the day, the woman's face played in my thoughts. I saw her turn her head to look for the right building, over and over. I replayed the look on her face as she drove. The day slipped by and I saw more of my mother in that face, until my memories had me believing that I'd actually seen my mom driving around town. I wanted to believe that I'm not that foolish: that I didn't really think it was my mother driving past me, but I couldn't shake the feeling that I'd seen her ghost.

In the four months since her death I've slowly been coming to terms with her illness and all that it took from her, and from us. I've been trying to remember more of the times we shared before she became ill, instead of the slow, agonizing decline that was her life for far too long. It's not easy. The reality is that Huntington's disease came to define her over the 12 years that she suffered. In the end, it was often what people saw first when she approached them, and what we saw too often, in place of the enormous personality that she'd once had.

Her walker; the messy, unfashionable clothes she wore; the toothless grin, because she hated her dentures; the vacant look in her eyes so much of the time: all of this replaced the mother I'd once felt so enmeshed with. It replaced the mother I adored, resented, struggled with and loved, the woman I tried to emulate and then tried to distance myself from. In the end, gone was her perfectionism: regarding her hair, her wardrobe, her overall appearance. Instead, she had settled for the simple goal of being as comfortable as possible, without concern for others' opinions. It's an attitude that so many of us claim we aspire to but, trust me, it can prove very different in real life.

Her walker, the messy, unfashionable clothes, the toothless grin, the vacant look: all of this replaced the mother I'd once felt so enmeshed with

For much of my life, I believed my mother worried too much about what other people thought. I thought that she was too focused on how she looked, what label she wore, standing out in the crowd. She was a business owner before many women had even figured out how to survive without a man. She was independent and smart about so many things, while missing some of the crucial things that would have made her life easier. She was stylish and charismatic; she was funny, playful, ballsy. She was the one who made so many of our family get-togethers an event, often the life of the party. She was sarcastic and wry, and she rarely missed a good line, all the while looking better than most people around her. Lilly Pulitzer skirts, silk blouses, the perfect shoe for each outfit, and her hair, make-up and nails were always impeccable. When she walked in a room everyone noticed.

When I was young, I resented her obsessive fascination with style and fashion. It was something she forced on us as well. Throughout elementary school, my mother insisted that I dress in styles that were better suited to *Vogue* and *Cosmo*, better suited to adults, than to the small town where we lived or the kid I was. Navy blue gauchos with "pop" daisies, paired with a kelly-green jacket-top, while my peers were wearing simple jumpers. In junior high I fought forever to get a pair of what was then the biggest craze among my peers: straight-leg boy's Levis. I was forbidden to wear them. "They're so boyish, so plain," she told me. Finally, in 9th grade, my pleading caused her to relent. I bought them with money I'd earned babysitting. As I walked awkwardly into the kitchen the first time I wore my still-stiff, powder blue Levis, she looked at me carefully and said sarcastically, "Hmm, they look comfortable too."

She was totally at a loss whenever she looked at my unpolished, often dirty, finger nails. "How can you walk around without a manicure?" I would roll my eyes and remind her that gardening and horseback riding, things I did daily until 10 years ago, were enemies to any manicure. She never bought my excuses.

I offered to have a friend come do her hair. She rolled her eyes and told me "It doesn't matter anymore."

As her Huntington's progressed and she began to lose one piece of herself after another, it was her lack of interest in her appearance that most startled me in the end. Right to the last days. Each time she showed up without a bra, or with food on her already faded, favorite black shirt, I was stumped. Each time her luxuriously thick silver hair stood up, unbrushed or unstyled, I had to resist the urge to grab a spritz bottle and a brush.

The tables turned. She hated that her appearance

bothered me. "Just leave me alone, Dawn," she'd say, tiny bits of her autonomy still intact. Only now do I see that my desperate desire to help her look good was my unconscious attempt to deny the end I knew was close, and that I was not ready for.

When I'd offered to have a friend come do her hair, as she lay in her hospice bed, days away from death, she rolled her eyes and told me "It doesn't matter anymore." But she died with perfect red polish on her toes, a striking contrast to her wasted body. She let my sister and I do her fingernails days before she died.

I bought her new clothes right up until the end, but she clung to a few items she'd come to love, and I came to loathe. "Why aren't you wearing the nice brown sweater I bought you?" I'd ask. "It's in the laundry," she always replied, sometimes avoiding my eyes, other times staring me down. I'm certain that she was still cognizant enough to calculate that that answer would shut me up. This reasoning, however, left me wondering why she didn't wear the brown sweater with food on it, instead of the old black shirt with food on it. Each time I went to her closet in frustration, the new items sat neglected on the shelves. When she died, I couldn't count how many of the things that I sent to the YWCA's Back to Work program were brand new. Many had never been worn. Honestly, it is at the least hopeful of me to think that she was still clear enough to willfully choose the older, rattier outfits just to push my buttons, and more likely delusional of me. Yet, many times that's exactly what I believed. I needed to believe that she wasn't completely gone in those last few years. I needed to believe that parts of her lay hidden in the body that suggested otherwise. While the dementia and ticks of Huntington's drove my mother, grief drove me.

Now I long for a few of those tangled interactions. Some days, I miss the vacant look and the ravaged body that was left, as much as I yearn for the vibrant mother of so many years ago. My frailer mother hugged me as if it would be the last time, each time she greeted me or said goodbye. Mostly it annoyed me, as I was simultaneously struggling to get her to the car, make dinner, or not engage in a discussion about her clothing choice. And even then, I knew that one day I'd regret my shortsightedness, my frustration and harsh judgment. I knew, even as the days were ticking by, that I would miss her and wish for at least one of those moments back. I knew all of that; but I guess I never really anticipated that I'd be seeing her ghost, that she'd come back to haunt me.

Football Saturdays

BY
DONNA K. BARRY

I AM A COLLEGE FOOTBALL FAN, mostly out of necessity, having been the minority gender at my house since 1976. Having a husband, two boys and no girls was great most of the time, but left me with the choice of (a) becoming a football fan so I'd have someone to talk to from August to January, or (b) not becoming a football fan, and having lots of time to do girl things by myself. I didn't want to miss a whole chunk of my children's growing up just because they were, well, boys, so I became sort of a football fan.

When my boys were younger I'd read *Sports Illustrated for Kids* while they were at school. When they got home and paged through the magazine, I'd be ready. I could talk football, and most sports with them, and not be left out. And it turned out to be fun.

As the kids became older it got easier. First, I had learned more by then and, second, they had other things they wanted to do besides talk to me, so I didn't have to keep up with quite so much. So I'd just read up on Michigan (the University of Michigan that is) and the Chicago Bears, and I'd be set. And then I'd follow my favorite quarterbacks because, while working hard to become a faux football fan, I'd actually found a few things I liked about football.

Then, something happened to up the ante. First-born son entered the University of Michigan and began to play in the marching band. Suddenly, I didn't just have to know about football, I had to go to it. Well, I didn't *have* to go, I *wanted* to: what mom wouldn't want to see her first-born child marching across the field at The Big House?

And so I went. I became the postal worker of football—through rain, snow, sleet, and dark of night,

I was there. Sometimes I had to slide a slab of ice off the bleacher before I could sit down. More than once I sat in driving rain, wearing that true fashion statement, the rain poncho. Suddenly, I owned more cold-weather gear than Edmund Hillary. I bought hand-warmers by the case. But it wasn't all cold work and no play. I got to go to the Rose Bowl with my whole family in 1998. And I got to spend countless hours with my boys as they were growing up, that I would have missed had I eschewed football for only girl things.

Today, I have a new football buddy. Grandson Zachary entered the world as we were heading down the highway to yet another Michigan game. As I sat shivering in the chilly wind, singing *Hail to the Victors* for the umpteenth time, I kept pulling out my phone to look at the picture of my sweet little newest Michigan fan. Before too long we'll be able to toss a little football, and talk about quarterbacks, the secondary, and interceptions.

I can't wait.

Ice Cream Odyssey

BY
GABI COATSWORTH

My HUSBAND IS an ice cream snob. It never occurred to me to wonder about this until the other day when I suggested going for an ice cream somewhere nearby, and Jay demurred, saying the only ice cream worth having was the one either 11 or 20 miles away. When did this fussiness begin? I'm thinking back to when I first arrived in America. It became very clear to me almost immediately that American cuisine had introduced three great things to the world: hamburgers, really interesting salads, and ice cream. Oh, we had ice cream in England, too, but it came wrapped in individual portions, either as vanilla ice cream bars (covered with chocolate) or in small paper cups, with a little wooden spade to eat it with.

So when I arrived in the US and was taken by my husband to a Baskin Robbins (32 flavors) I was astonished and delighted. I made it a goal to try all the flavors worth tasting. Mint chocolate chip? How sophisticated. Nutty coconut? An inspired recipe. Butter pecan? It contained those nuts I'd only heard about back in England. And then Jamoca, my true love. My husband, on the other hand, stuck to the only flavor he really liked: Pralines 'n' Cream.

Soon, however, the siren song of Häagen Dazs was heard throughout the land. Their ice cream was better, richer and more imaginative, said Jay.

I loved Swiss Almond, Amaretto Almond Crunch and Rum Raisin. Jay stuck to Macadamia Nut, until they introduced Macadamia Brittle, the king of ice creams, according to Jay. There was one drawback. Those macadamia flavors were hard to find—something to do with the macadamia crop in Hawaii being too expensive.

But Jay was not despondent for too long.

We bought a little house in New Hampshire, and the local ice cream there, was, of course, Ben & Jerry's. I approved of this ice cream, made by a couple of hippies who invented flavors like Cherry Garcia, Wavy Gravy and Phish Food. Jay was happy again—even if they retired one flavor, there was always another. So Southern Pecan Pie was followed by Rainforest Crunch and then Karamel Sutra.

Then tragedy struck. The small ice cream parlor in our town stopped serving Ben & Jerry's. They still sold ice cream, but it didn't have the oomph Jay needed.

So Southern Pecan Pie was followed by Rainforest Crunch and then Karamel Sutra

Last summer, while driving in farm country after picking blueberries, Jay swerved off the road. He'd seen a sign, he said. I thought maybe he'd had some sort of epiphany. The sign, a cutout of an ice cream cone, advertised the Walpole Creamery.

"We deserve a reward for picking all those blueberries," he said, enjoying a new flavor, Caramel Cashew Chip.

And he's been going back ever since. (The blueberries have long since stopped being an excuse.)

"This is, hands down, the best ice cream ever," he announced recently.

Being a bit older now and, he assures me, much wiser, Jay has a backup plan in the event that the Walpole Creamery ice cream is not available. Only 20 miles away, he knows a little spot called the Scoop, where he swears the ice cream is as good.

I don't worry about finding the perfect ice cream for myself. Dear old Häagen Dazs has produced a coffee ice cream that comes in small paper cups, with a little plastic spoon to eat it with, reminding me of the ice cream I ate living in England. That's what I love about ice cream—some things never change.

Socks

BY
BARBARA YOUNGER

Socks don't lead
An easy life.
Missing partners,
Sweaty feet, and
Hours squinched
In tight quarters,
Yet I never hear
My socks complain.
Maybe I should be
More like socks.
Complaining less,
Absorbing more,
And ever ready to
Step into shoes
For the next adventure.

Clotheslines

BY
PATTI WINKER

I GREW UP IN WISCONSIN where the world comes alive in May. It was the first month that we could start relying on a few nice warm days and when Mom could trust that the laundry on the clothesline would actually dry instead of freeze.

Most might find it hard to feel nostalgic about any kind of laundry, let alone lugging heavy baskets outside to dry on lines. Line drying the wash is hard work and not often reliable. Mom watched the sky, constantly on the lookout for ominous dark clouds. There were no guarantees that all her hard work wouldn't end up back in the house, soaking wet.

Mom passed along the rules of proper clothesline procedures: hang pants and shirts to the street, sheets next, then unmentionables behind the sheets, then the towels, then more shirts and pants. And always hang the wash in the morning, and never leave clothes on the line after sunset.

I knew all these rules growing up, but I remember more the art, the music, and yes, the fun of the clothesline. I love the arranged patterns of laundry catching a breeze and getting warm with the sun's rays. I hear the music in the sheets snapping as a good strong wind grabs them.

I remember Mom with clothespins in her apron pocket, arranging the sheets, towels, and clothes strung together in neat rows, catching the wind, billowing like windsocks at an airport.

For us, the clothesline provided a playground. We ran through those rows and rows of sheets and towels as they whipped around in the wind. Mom would come back out with another basket of laundry just in time to holler, "go play someplace else!"

There's nothing like sun-dried bed sheets and pillowcases. Now, when I toss and turn at night, I long for sheets dried by the sun.

My Son, The Rocker

BY
CHRIS ROSEN

"**D**ID YOU JUMP and have cookies?" my toddler David greeted his father. His little body sailed towards the ceiling, jumping on the bed as his dad came home from the hospital.

Bob would always begin his transition to home by taking off his tie and recounting his day. Our seven-year-old daughter, big sister Jess, would invariably ask, "Who did you see today who hurt themselves, Daddy?"

But her persistent younger brother wanted to

know exactly how much fun his daddy had had that day. Intuitively he knew, if work was fun, then it wasn't work at all.

David James was born in the middle of a heat wave in The Berkshires. Gladioli were in bloom. While I was dreaming of flying on a trapeze at the Big Apple Circus, he began his entry into the Big Top of Life. He was loud and lovely, a delicious baby boy in every way. His arms were like ears of corn, the kind you pretend to eat. I called him my perpetual motion machine; he never looked back, he'd let go of my hand and walk into danger: an open stairwell, the ocean or pre-school.

Rollerblades, ice skates and sticks littered our front hall. Anything to make him go faster. Only the promise of a guitar, when Dave turned six, could slow him down. He endured two years of violin lessons—our Welsh Corgis would howl as he played—in order to win his first Fender, the guitar that he has rarely put down.

Summer birthdays included everyone at the beach. One August day, he was searching for lost treasure during a birthday treasure hunt, and then the next he was playing in front of thousands at

Lollapalooza music festival when the crowd sang *Happy Birthday* to him.

"He's living the Dream," Bob likes to say.

Our son, the guitarist with Parlor Mob, found out the secret to life: how to jump and have his cookies too.

To My Sister

BY
GABI COATSWORTH

They told me there was an end to every pain
They insisted on it, the grief counselors.
But no one can structure my sorrow,
I have to sculpt that piece of flint myself.

Years later, sudden and sharp—a chiseled
arrowhead—
The longing for you takes me by surprise.

I've done enough, I want to tell you—
I've done my best with the son you left behind.
Why can't you take over, now?
Because you're dead, I scream into the silence,
and one day, your son will be as old as you, then
older.

But when I see our son I remember how you
were:

the way he scowls when I call him on something
the rueful look he has when I catch him out,
his helpless laughter when I crack him up,
the way he stands, his back curved, weight on
one leg.

It's you—
And it's not.

My sculpture is still made of sorrow's stone
but the edges are a little smoother, softer, now.

A Weighty Issue

BY
LEAH R. SINGER

WEIGHT IS A TOUGH TOPIC for me. It's been an emotional issue that's been a part of my core from a very young age. But it's one that I've recognized and embraced, especially now that I have a daughter for whose health I am responsible.

I was never a skinny girl. I was not chubby either. I was average, maybe slightly more so, but certainly not obese. I became aware of weight and dieting from my mother. Not a large woman, she seemed to always be complaining about her weight and was always on some sort of diet.

I remember when I was six or seven years old, sitting with my family watching *Charlotte's Web* on television. For whatever reason, I blurted out: "Mom, it's a pig. Like you."

I realized quickly that I'd hurt her feelings. But I was puzzled because I distinctly remember hearing my mother refer to herself with such a derogatory term. A six-year-old wouldn't know that's how to be cruel. I was just repeating what I'd heard from her. But it was a stark realization that something was not good about being overweight (which, again, she was not).

When I was in the 6th grade, I remember being weighed at the doctor's office and the number on the scale was just slightly over 100 pounds. My parents later told me that was too much for a 6th-grader to be weighing and I needed to watch what I ate (whatever that meant to an 11-year-old).

I remember finding a sleeveless dress to wear to my grandfather's wedding when he remarried. I was 13 years old. My parents said I needed to lose five pounds to wear the dress. I was constantly worried about the perception of what I put in my mouth. Whether it was more than one slice of pizza or dessert, I always felt like I was being watched.

The worst was when I was a freshman in high school. My parents noticed that I ate from a bag of Cheetos in our house. This after-school snack led to a several hours long conversation about the fact that, they believed, I was overweight and needed to go on a diet. Now I would ask why Cheetos were even in the house if they were so bad, but that's beside the point. They put me on a reduced carbohydrate diet. I felt like a disappointment.

Physical activity was never something the entire family engaged in for fun or health. Instead, exercise was punishment for being overweight. My parents told me to exercise because I needed to lose weight. And the more they nagged, the more I resisted. My dad ran two miles a day at the high school football field and one of my sisters played soccer and basketball from an early age. My mother never exercised. When we had dogs, they never got walked.

Somehow, I realized that though I took their criticisms to heart, their attitude toward food and dieting wasn't normal. I knew I wasn't a bad person and they weren't right.

My attitude toward exercise and food changed during my freshmen year of college. It was second semester and I put on a few pounds. All freshmen living on-campus do. I remember feeling gross and miserable, when a close friend took me to a gym for the first time. The gym intrigued me—you could run, bike, or do the elliptical; it didn't matter. After we worked out, I assumed I would skip eating that evening, or just eat something tiny like a salad. My friend told me that was so unhealthy and that the body needed food; but good food. I'd never heard this before. I was so used to cutting calories and carbs that I never realized how to eat right. We went to dinner together at the school cafeteria where she showed me what good foods I should be eating.

It has taken me some 30+ years to get to a place where I'm finally at peace with who I am

From then on, things changed for me. I bought my first gym membership that spring and began to exercise regularly. I learned how to eat right; that spring and summer was the first time I lost weight through my own motivation. It felt good to be healthy.

It has taken me some 30+ years to get to a place

where I'm finally at peace with who I am, the foods I eat, and the realization that (for me) the only way to really maintain a healthy body is to exercise.

I'm not saying I have not struggled. Right now, my body challenge has to do with making peace with my shape and size post-baby. I'm learning to deal with a new reality that I may never look the same as before my pregnancy. It's definitely a challenge. Of course, I'd love to wear all my smaller clothes and look the way I did before Sophie came into my life. But I take each day as I can and embrace natural steps to make that happen.

Now that I'm a mother of a daughter, these issues of weight and exercise have come full circle. My goal with Sophie is that I teach her about nutrition, and make exercise fun to do. I want to teach Sophie how to maintain a healthy mind, body and soul. I hope with those key values and support, her journey through this weight-obsessed society will be easier than mine.

Before Helmets

BY
PATTI WINKER

I GREW UP in a world before play dates, kiddie leashes, helmets, cell phones, "may contain choking hazards", hand sanitizer, "adult supervision required", and guarded entrances.

My parents had a crazy notion to raise 11 kids on the banks of a river below a dam which formed a lake, next to the railroad tracks and trestle over the river, and down the road from a railroad switching yard. Mom and Dad believed in "either sink or swim," which in our case was quite a literal expression.

We grew up unleashed and ran in packs from early morning until after dark.

All summer we put on our swimsuits as soon as we got up and headed for the lake, jumping off an old rusted barrel that was half submerged. After swimming all day, we returned home via the railroad trestle, stopping to jump into the river and swim to the dock. We took old inner tubes up to the dam and rafted into the white water. When we got tired, we walked home, barefoot, along the highway. Then we rode our bikes for miles along winding country roads.

When fall came we raked up big leaf piles and dove in. We then set the leaf piles on fire, and stood around late into the night adding tinder we gathered as we cleaned up the yard. As the garden ripened and whatever was left rotted, we pelted any and all unsuspecting targets with tomatoes.

In the winter, we dug tunnels in the snow banks that the plows left along the road and crawled deep inside those caves. We skated on the pond until dark or found the highest hill and hit the slopes with our sleds or large pieces of cardboard.

As soon as spring arrived, we were on the road

again, jumping rope. We waited for the ice to begin to break in the lake and then dared each other to take the first polar bear dip.

Today I wear a helmet when I ride my bike. I don't leave the house without my cell phone. I've taken some turns toward caution, and I understand why my grandchildren have too. But I still miss the time before helmets.

You Had a Good Run, Grandma

BY
DONNA K. BARRY

MY MOTHER DIED AT 85. She had a long life, most of it healthy despite a robust smoking habit, some of it good, some not, but overall a life that was varied and interesting. She was born of immigrant parents and grew up in a working class neighborhood of mostly Polish, Slovenian, and others of eastern European descent. Her father worked in a factory. Her mother stayed home raising kids, making chicken soup with homemade noodles, and *poticca* (poppy-seed bread) on special occasions, hanging her laundry on the line to dry while chatting over the fence to neighbors, and shopping at a neighborhood market, where you handed your list to the clerk behind the counter and they filled your order for you.

My mother said they were "lucky" during the Depression, because her father had a part-time job as a night watchman in a factory, while many other dads had nothing. Her growing-up years are portrayed in pictures of her with her friends, sledding down a neighborhood hill, standing sweetly next to boyfriends—almost all dressed in army uniforms—and arm in arm with girlfriends, walking down the streets of Chicago or posing with the stone lions in front of the Art Institute. She quit high school in 11th grade to help support her family and worked in a factory making Karo syrup. Maybe that's why her hearing became so bad in later years, as there was no Occupational Safety and Health Administration to protect workers then. Later, as an adult, she proudly completed her GED*, not because she had to, but because

*High school examinations

she felt incomplete without that diploma, even though she grew up in a time when many people, especially women, did not complete school past the 8th grade.

She left her family in Chicago to move, with her new husband, to a farm in Michigan. Although she grew up a city girl, she traded it all for love, to make pickles, gather eggs, and sell tomato seedlings from our little greenhouse. She raised three children without the benefit of disposable diapers, ready-made formula or an automatic clothes washer. She canned jam, hung clothes outside to dry and spent an entire day each week ironing. Her only phone was a black desk model on a party line. Her TV received two channels. She styled her hair with pin curls and gave her daughters hideous home perms.

She was the only mom who taught her daughters how to play hopscotch *and* poker. She carried cigarettes in her purse next to pictures of her grandchildren. She could curse like a sailor and sweet-talk the priest, all on the same day. One of her fondest memories was the day her grandchildren took her to a casino.

People describe her as sometimes funny, sometimes fun, but always feisty. She was not afraid to speak her mind. I always heard about it if she didn't like my clothes or hair or what I was doing, and not just as a teenager, but as an adult too. Her motto was "don't go to any trouble," yet she made sure we went to all kinds of trouble when she wanted us to. She was too impatient to ever wait in a line, but patient enough to comfort us through our childhood illnesses and boyfriend dramas. She deferred decision making to her husband but, later, as a widow, gained confidence to hire a roofer and plumber, get her car serviced and learn how to drive through the car wash.

She was determined to stay in her own home until she died and made sure we all felt miserable and abused when we "made her" move to our local hospice. As we all whispered our goodbyes to her that Christmas day night, I think my youngest son said it best. He leaned into her ear and said "You had a good run, Grandma, you had a good run."

No Help Needed:
A Mother's Chagrin

BY
LISA K. WINKLER

PILES ARE GROWING in the basement. Like the Sorcerer's Apprentice's magic broom, splitting and multiplying nonstop, items seem to appear that weren't there minutes ago. A scene, I imagine, in dens, living rooms, front halls, basements and garages in countless homes across the nation.

The new foam mattress topper. A new mattress pad. New clothes. New boots. Stacks of freshly laundered t-shirts. A tennis racquet waiting to be restrung. New tennis sneakers. The winter coat and sweaters packed from the dry cleaners. Extra hangers. A fan. Duffle bags soon to be filled.

And my stomach is starting to ache. My daughter is returning to college in two days. I offered to drive with her and fly back. This year, she wants to take herself; there's not enough room in the car for either a friend with his things or me. So I won't even make her bed; a ritual I felt left a "mom loves you" stamp on her room. It makes saying goodbye easier.

Her freshman year, we drove her in the old mini-van. We set up her room, (I made her bed), and hung towel bars and a mirror. Last year, we each took three-hour shifts at the wheel and again helped her unpack. And I made her bed.

I remember seeing the television movie *Eleanor & Franklin* years ago. Jane Alexander played the First Lady. At one point, when their six offspring were dashing out, she said: "We're always saying goodbye to the children."

The line stuck, though I didn't have any kids of my own then.

Now I know how she felt.

Pondering Good and Evil

BY
BARBARA YOUNGER

GOOD AND EVIL. Often, it's easy to know the difference. To decide. To choose. "Always do what's right," was one of my father's trademark lines. But then, there are the in-between cases, the not-so-sure situations, the maybe yes or maybe no.

Fudge Prayer
Dear God,
I can't decide if fudge,
Is good or evil.
Cocoa beans, sugar, rich butter,
Confection of good delight
Or calories of evil to the body temple.
The fudge is gone,
Swallowed,
Not unlike the cat and canary.
And now I offer this
Grateful Prayer of Thanksgiving
Or this humble Prayer of Repentance.
Amen and Amen.

Up, Up and Away

BY
CHRIS ROSEN

Miss Bean, our two-year-old shelter dog, started barking furiously on the deck while I was finishing making the pesto. Looking out towards the mountains, I saw why. A beautiful hot air balloon was floating over the valley and heading towards us! If it wasn't for our trees, it might have landed on our hill.

I remembered our hot air balloon ride after we first moved to Virginia from New Jersey. It was our

25th wedding anniversary present and something I'd always wanted to do.

The cows ran under trees to escape the dreaded fire-spurting, floating, monster balloon; egrets glided along our basket's wake and tractors spit out hay rolls underneath us. Worst of all, I didn't know where we would land. We were at the mercy of the wind. Our pilot tried to gently reassure us, while looking down for an empty field.

I nearly panicked as we started descending, skimming trees looking for open space in preparation for a landing. Then suddenly, I let go.

Riding on the wind helped with my moving South, with leaving my friends and the state I'd called home for most of my life.

I WAS SO READY for those balloon voyagers with champagne and a bowl of pasta pesto primavera, but they flew on.

Tart From Seville

BY
STACEY E. CARON

I LOVE TO TRAVEL. Every night I travel to Italy, Spain and France—via my computer. I guess you can call me an armchair traveler. I could tell you every good hotel in Piedmont and fabulous chateau in Bordeaux. What airline flies direct from New York to Milan and how many miles between Paris and Provence via the high-speed train.

I am always planning my next vacation years in advance. Though we only take one trip a year, I make it worthwhile. I do as much research as possible, using Google Maps, websites, reviews, blogs, and word of mouth to find the best places to eat, best neighborhoods to stay in and explore, and best places to visit. It makes for a memorable vacation.

Try it. French, Italian or Spanish. Open a good bottle of wine from the region, a cheese from the same region and make a simple recipe from that place and, for an evening, you are transported to somewhere special. I have just saved you a lot of money on airfare. Recently, I went to Seville, Spain, and woke up in New Jersey. Serrano ham and Manchego cheese from Spain with a Spanish fig spread. The recipe below calls for fig spread, such as Dalmatia from Greece which has an orange flavor. I had fig preserves with some dried California figs, so I used that. Use whatever you find.

TORTA DI SEVILLA

1 sheet defrosted frozen puff pastry
2 onions, thinly sliced
Olive oil
2 tbsp balsamic vinegar
1 tbsp fresh thyme leaves
1 tsp brown sugar

Salt and pepper
Approx 4 tbsp fig preserves or fig spread
mixed with chopped dried figs
4 oz Serrano (Spanish ham) or prosciutto
4 oz Manchego or Iberico cheese, thinly sliced
Chopped walnuts for the top (optional)

Caramelize the onions. In a heavy skillet, cook onions in some olive oil on low heat for about 15 minutes until golden. Add brown sugar, thyme and splash of balsamic vinegar in the last few minutes. Set aside to cool. Season with salt and pepper. Roll out dough into a large rectangle and fit onto a parchment-lined baking sheet. Spread some of fig spread in center of puff pastry, leaving a 1" border on each side. Drape slices of Serrano ham over fig spread and dried figs (if using) and then some slices of the Spanish cheese. Spoon cooled onion mixture over ham and cheese and sprinkle with chopped walnuts. Fold up border to create edges to hold filling in. Bake for 20 to 25 minutes at 375°F.

Bon Voyage!

Shrimping

BY
GABI COATSWORTH

I'M RUNNING AROUND THE BEACH chasing my granddaughters, aged two and three. They are laughing and trying to keep their hair out of their eyes as they head for the waves. This might not be a problem, except that, although it's sunny and unseasonably warm, it is November and they've been shedding their clothes as they run, leaving little pink and purple discards across the sand.

I CAN SEE MYSELF at about four years old. My parents, my twin sisters and I were spending the summer at my grandparents' house by the sea. We spent hours on the beach, paddling barefoot in the shallows, holding firmly to my father's hand. To keep his trousers dry, he rolled them halfway up his calves. He stooped to hold my hand, and I knew he would never let it go. My mother sat on a striped blanket not too far away, shading her eyes from the afternoon sun as she watched us and smiled. She was surrounded by four pairs of sandals: my father's large ones, and ours. My twin sisters used to chase each other around the rock pools, their flaxen curls flying around their heads. They were two years older than me, and I can hear them singing and yelling to each other. The three of us wore ruched bathing costumes, with little straps that tied behind our necks. Mine was pink, the twins' blue and green.

I could smell the salt as the sea edged towards us, getting closer with each wave. Daddy would stretch out his arms and take in an enormous breath of 'good sea air' before letting it out again. The waves weren't too big, and they made me curl up my toes and wiggle my feet further down into the sand as the waves retreated again. Daddy would pick up a tiny crab with his free hand, and crouch down to show it to me. I looked in his eyes and he was smiling. I knew the crab wouldn't hurt me so long as he was there.

I used to wonder sometimes if the sea would ever come back again. I would look out of my bedroom window, under the eaves of Granny and Grandpa's house, and sometimes the sea would be right up, covering the pebble beach, and at other times I couldn't see it at all; it was so far away. All I could see was sand, stretching away to the end of the world. It felt a bit scary, but there is one wonderful thing about sand like that. In the summer, after we'd had supper, my father would take us out shrimping before bedtime.

What we did find in our nets, and this made me forget my yearning for shrimp, were shells, crabs and the occasional mermaid's purse

We'd walk down the drive toward the main road in front of the house. Holding hands in a straggling chain, we would cross the road after repeating the incantation: "Look right, look left, look right again. If all clear, quick march." This last was, I suspect, my mother's variation on "cross the road". She had been in the army, after all.

Rays from the setting sun lit the beach, illuminating the wet sand that rippled away to the horizon. A row of small huts, brightly painted like colored building blocks, separated the beach from the grey world inland. These were the bathing huts, and they consisted of one room with no windows and a tiny wooden porch.

Ours was the green one, and we used it for changing in and out of our swimsuits, as well as for storing our buckets and spades, towels and deck chairs. We collected our shrimp nets and buckets, left our sandals in the hut, and made our way slowly across the sand, avoiding sharp stones. Our father would remind us to stay between the two breakwaters we could see to the right and left, stretching down towards the sea. I loved the feel of that cool, wet sand. I curled my toes into it before picking up my feet to watch my footprints sink back into the beach.

We pushed our shrimp nets along the sand in the shallows. The net was essentially a wooden pole with a flat board across the end of it forming a T-shape. The flat board was designed to scoop up the shrimp that would dig themselves into the sand when they heard footsteps approaching (or so said my mother, trying to explain how it was that we rarely caught any). A net attached to the board would collect them and we would then tip them into our buckets.

I think I may have caught a total of six shrimp, ever. And these were not American shrimp, these were English ones, about half an inch long, and sand-colored, so that they were hard to see, even if I did catch them.

What we did find in our nets, and this made me forget my yearning for shrimp, were shells, crabs and the occasional mermaid's purse. Our father would pick the crabs gently out of the net, and turn them upside down to make us count their waving claws and look at their peculiar eyes on stalks. Sometimes he would let us carry them for a little while in our buckets, but eventually he would explain that we had to let these crabs go back to their mothers, and it was time for us to go back to our mother, too.

We would toil back up the beach, carrying our buckets full of shells and seaweed, quieter now, and yawning, ready for sleep.

I STILL GO DOWN TO THE SEA whenever I can, even though those days vanished forever when I was 12, and my father died. I take my granddaughters to the beach and paddle barefoot with them in the shallows, holding their hands, looking for crabs.

Sweetie's Fudge Shoppe: Not So Sweet!

BY
PATTI WINKER

NOT EVERYONE is meant to be a shopkeeper. Even if the situation appears to be perfect, you have to know yourself really well before you dive into that kind of enterprise. And, there are some things you just won't learn until you are on the job.

This is the story of Sweetie's Fudge Shoppe.

Back in the early 1990s, we owned a video store, which my husband managed. I worked at the county social services office. My husband came from a long line of shopkeepers; it suited him fine.

One day, having had it with my government job, I decided I wanted to be a shopkeeper too. When the fudge shop next door to the video store came up for sale, I jumped. It seemed perfect: the business was solid and the building sound, with an apartment behind where we could live. We knocked down the wall between the stores and created a video-fudge shop.

I left the job I'd held for four years. I learned how to make beautiful pans of fudge. I made sheets of pecan turtles, lovingly constructing each one with my own hands, decorating each with a little "S" swirl on the chocolate top for "Sweetie's." Chocolate-covered cherries and fudge-filled chocolate cups. I mixed batch after batch, late at night, and lined them up attractively in the display cases.

Then came the morning, time to open the shop.

And in came the customers.

I couldn't deal with sending my creations away, to be eaten and destroyed, even if I was being paid.

My husband, in contrast, loved seeing the boxes and bags going out the door every day. He became puzzled at my increasingly sullen mood as business improved. The more fudge and turtles I sold, the darker my days.

I don't know if anything could have prepared me for the way I felt. In my mind, I knew I was being silly. I knew selling my goods was the idea behind having a shop. But, in my heart, I knew I was not, nor ever would be, a shopkeeper. I owned the candy shop for almost five years. During those years, I tried many things, including hiring someone to wait on the customers so I could stay behind the scenes and just make the confections. With your own business, customers want to see you.

We sold the candy and video store, put the cats in the car, and moved to Florida. We knew we just wanted to try something new and live where it's warm and enjoy the beach.

Thankfully, someone with the heart of a shopkeeper bought it and is making fudge and turtles for customers.

Bringing Back Dad

BY
BARBARA YOUNGER

M Y FATHER DIED, still exuberant at 92, while taking what was supposed to be a short nap. My mother went to wake him and he was gone. Still in his bed, but gone.

I had a moment when I realized that my father was really dead. I stepped in the study and saw, on the bookshelves, his CDs.

Dad adored music. He listened to "God of Our Fathers" or "A Mighty Fortress" on Sunday mornings before church. He blasted John Philip

Sousa on the Fourth of July and Ray Conniff at Christmas.

"Take some of his CDs," my mom said, and I did.

But I didn't play them. I couldn't.

I had a few dreams that my father wasn't really dead. He called us. "I'm fine," he said, standing in a phone booth. "I'll be home soon."

But he didn't come home.

And for about six months I had the strange feeling that I could bring him back.

But Dad didn't reappear. And his CDs sat on my kitchen shelf. Silent.

But then one day I played one. And then another and another. Gordon Lightfoot. *Phantom of the Opera*. *Mama Mia*. Simon and Garfunkel. Peter, Paul and Mary. *South Pacific*. The Drifters. Mitch Miller. Willie Nelson. Glen Campbell. John Denver.

Dad in the music! Dad in my kitchen!

Not in the same way, but still, back to life.

Duress? Distress? Dial!

BY
MADELINE G. TAYLOR

WHEN I FIRST JOINED Facebook, I wrote my "25 Random Things" list to tell readers more about me.

Communicating on the telephone with my siblings came to mind. I wrote: "I speak to my sister, Lisa, four times a day. I speak to my sister, Naomi, four times a week and I speak to my brother, David, four times a year."

I have no animosity toward my brother. Growing up, we were really close. We're 11 months apart and shared a room until we were nine and ten, seeing no reason to be separated except when other people thought so.

It's just that as adults and as parents, we seem to have less to talk about and I have so much more to say to my sisters, especially on the phone. We can chat about every mundane tidbit of our lives. We can multi-task while sharing our stories. We'll be on the phone while cooking in our respective kitchens, sharing the steps and outcomes of our endeavors, wishing we lived closer for tastings. We scrub the tub, load the dishwasher, or make a salad without missing a syllable.

We talk about everything and nothing. I need advice on SAT tutoring for my daughter. Lisa needs to know why her banana cake doesn't come out like mine. Naomi shares the latest news about her kids and our cousins.

The endless hours I spend with my sisters talking on the phone sometimes make it seem we're doing no more than listening to each other breathe. Not literally of course, but if I were to tell all that we talk about, no one would see the point.

Phone conversations with my brother are limited

to a single topic or query; that covered, there's no need to linger. Mission accomplished. Hang up. Move on. In person, it's totally different; we can talk for hours. Only our phone conversations are brisk.

I worry about my daughter. As an only child, who will she call when she needs to know if she can substitute margarine for butter in her stuffing recipe? Or when she has kids of her own, who will advise her on how to care for them, steer them and provide for them?

Of course, hers is the texting generation. She doesn't make phone calls unless it's to her dear Mom. She knows, from reading my list of 25 Random Things, that (#23), texting is not for me.

When I Lied
About My Age

BY
DONNA K. BARRY

WHAT WOULD YOU DO to land a summer job?
Now that I'm at an age where most women
do lie about their age, I don't.

The one time I did lie about my age was when I
was 17 and had just graduated from high school. I
wanted to get a summer job so I would have some
money to take to college, but everywhere I looked
for a job that wasn't babysitting or picking up trash
in the park, the employer wanted someone 18 or

older. I wasn't going to turn 18 until December and I needed money immediately.

After being rejected repeatedly for being too young, I finally figured out that I could lie and just say I was 18. Either it was way easier to lie about your age back then, or the employer was not very thorough, because I got away with it. I don't remember having to show ID, or maybe I did but covered up my date of birth with my thumb.

So what was the job I wanted so badly that I lied to get? It was calling people to apply for a Montgomery Ward credit card. It was one of the original telemarketing jobs.

Was it worth it? I hated every minute of the job, but did earn enough money to take to school, convinced my boyfriend to apply for a card, and I am to this day exceedingly polite to telemarketers when I tell them I'm not interested.

Food = Love

BY
STACEY E. CARON

MY FIRST EXPERIENCE WITH LOVE and food (and the love of food) started when I was a small child.

My grandma Dorothy provided both.

I couldn't wait to go to my grandparents' house in Queens, New York, to get lots of hugs and kisses, a toy, and best of all, a huge meal, always starting with cantaloupe or grapefruit (depending on the season), a salad, then three main dishes. She worked with my grandfather at their fabric store and took

Wednesdays off to clean house, shop and cook for the week, so Sunday was really her only day off and she still cooked all day.

She always made my favorites—stuffed cabbages with meat and rice in a sweet sauce with raisins. Always chopped liver with egg and onion served on a wedge of iceberg lettuce for the holidays. There were always dried fruits and nuts out on the table for nibbling. I would eat until my stomach hurt.

My best memory of my grandmother was of an elegant woman with fancy clothes, hair and makeup always done up, wearing a housecoat or shift all the time. If you didn't ask for second helpings, her standard line was "What's the matter? You didn't like it?"

She had an ongoing thing with my husband; always as we were leaving she would say, "Henry, I made you a little something to take home," and out came a large aluminum pan of either homemade baked beans with hot dogs baked inside, or nicely wrapped meatloaves made specially for him.

Food = Love.

My grandmother has been gone for about 10 years. I think of her often as I am cooking for large numbers of people in my tiny kitchen. But she had a great saying, which rings true: "If there is room in your heart, then there is room in your home."

For me, food has always been about love and caring about the people that are the recipients of that meal. So, you better ask for seconds and thirds and know that I love you!

Saying "I Do" to an Interfaith Wedding

BY
LEAH R. SINGER

IT HAS BEEN 11 YEARS since my husband, Bryan, and I said, "I do." It was a beautiful wedding. We stood under a chuppah* that was adorned with flowers, and there was just enough of a breeze to keep the July evening from being too warm.

While the wedding was certainly lovely and, more importantly, our marriage is still strong, getting to the chuppah was not an easy task. Especially because Bryan and I were an interfaith couple looking to

* Chuppah: wedding canopy

plan a wedding that was welcoming to our families and held to our own religious beliefs.

I was raised in what I'd call a culturally Jewish family, but certainly not religious. We celebrated the Jewish holidays at home, but never went to synagogue. As I went to college and grew older, Judaism became much more important to me and I started to seek out ways to bring Judaism into my life.

Bryan's family was Catholic and, like me, acknowledged holidays and little else. Bryan minored in religious studies in college so he was naturally curious when we began dating.

Why does religion suddenly become important during lifecycle events as it did for my parents? When I told my parents we had found the most beautiful outdoor venue that was only available Saturday afternoons, they were shocked. "You can't get married on Saturday!" my dad said. "Jews don't marry on the Sabbath."

Because we were never raised religiously, I honestly had never heard this rule.

Our quest to find a celebrant who would marry us was the first interfaith wedding challenge. We knew we wanted someone symbolic, not a justice of the peace, or a friend that was ordained for the day. My parents pressured me to have a rabbi marry us. As a non-Jew, Bryan wasn't too keen on this idea. When I first tried explaining this to my parents, they could not understand why Bryan would be uncomfortable with that. Not until I said, "How would you feel if we had a priest?" did they understand.

The fact that Bryan was not Jewish posed a problem for the Jewish clergy we approached. Very few in the Reform community would conduct the ceremony, especially on a Saturday. I spoke to a retired cantor who considered marrying us, only if we agreed to raise our children Jewish. While that was likely the course our lives would take, this was a very personal and private decision. Bryan and I were unwilling to make that promise to anyone other than ourselves.

Finally, we found a rabbi with a local Humanistic Jewish congregation who agreed to marry us. She was wonderful and made all guests—Jewish and non—feel welcome and included.

The next hurdle was what the ceremony would

"look like." Bryan and I both agreed to a chuppah and the breaking of the glass. But actual Hebrew language was something we had to negotiate. Bryan wasn't comfortable having parts of his wedding ceremony in a language he, and half the guests, didn't understand. So we compromised, reciting Jewish prayers in English and having his uncle read a verse from the New Testament.

We didn't dance the Hora or say Motzi* over the bread. We also didn't light unity candles and recite Christian prayers in our ceremony. This wedding was for Bryan and me. It was more about us coming together as a couple—to start a marriage—than it was about religion.

* Hora: celebratory circle dance. Motzi: blessing

Last Goodbyes

BY
BARBARA CHAPMAN

I HAVE THE DREAM JOB. I work for a hospice. I immerse myself in the life of someone who is in the process of making that final surrender and in the lives of the loved ones gathered at the bedside: haggard, sleep deprived, and in tremendous emotional pain.

I am often asked how I could do this kind of work because it is so sad. I tell them. Yes, it's sad but also a time of great honesty and vulnerability. I am invited into the tight circle of a family when they are spent. No one cares what they look like; no one remembers when they last ate. I plunge into the midst of it. It is an honor.

Take Merrill. He is listening to his favorite country western singer, Johnny Cash. In the final stages of Huntington's chorea, Merrill's body flails around in his bed uncontrollably. I sit beside him and initiate the same conversation I have had with him for several weeks. He doesn't recognize me, so the conversation is always new. "Merrill", I say, "Is it true that you were a paratrooper in the Korean War?"

> Hospice is not a place so much as it is a philosophy. It is a place to rest, to take shelter.

Merrill looks frantically around the room, his body reacting to a misfiring in his brain. "Yes," he says.

"Why on God's green earth would you jump out of a perfectly good airplane?"

A stillness overcomes him. He looks me in the eye, smiles and says, "Brave guy!" For that instant, we connect. His family members laugh and the mood in the room lightens.

Later I speak with Merrill's family and coach

them in the ABCs of dying and what to expect. I tell them that often times a dying person will wait for his family to arrive before he lets go. Or sometimes the person waits for his loved ones to leave. In Merrill's case, he waited for them to go for dinner and he passed in his sleep. I was there. I told his wife, two sons and daughter that he wasn't in pain and that their presence in the earlier hours of the day helped Merrill to complete his journey.

Hospice is not a place so much as it is a philosophy. It is a place to rest, to take shelter. In my job as a patient care liaison, I visit private homes, hospitals, and nursing homes to promote and teach a way of treating life and death as a natural occurrence.

I remember my first patient, Lori. For quite some time, she retained a good part of her fine motor skills. Lori and I would spend a few hours three times a week playing with the clay, chatting.

A former cook, she was interested in talking about meal preparation. I showed Lori a picture of a blueberry pie. "Oh. I know how to make that," she said.

"Show me, Lori. I have never made a blueberry pie."

"Well, it isn't all that difficult. You need your

dough to be just right, so you don't want to overwork it. Then you dump the carrots in the pan with a piece of shin beef. I've made it a million times."

"Do you mind if I write down what you have told me? We could make a cookbook! I'll cut the picture out, you can glue it on this paper and I will write down the recipe for you."

The day came when Lori was actively dying. I got to her bedside before her daughter, Georgiana. When Georgiana arrived, she talked to her mother even though Lori could no longer speak. "Mom, tomorrow I'll bring some flowers from the garden. Mom loves her garden, don't you, Mom? She's always out there picking flowers or vegetables to make something. You should see her garden, Barb … it's …"

I reach over and take Georgiana's hand, "Honey, I think she's gone."

Georgiana was so caught up chatting that she hadn't noticed the change in Lori's breathing. The long pause, then the huge final breath. Georgiana screamed. She draped herself over her mother's body and wailed. Nurses arrived. Lori was pronounced dead. I told Georgiana that I would be right outside the door. I left her to spend some final moments with her mom.

After someone dies, the loss is with the survivors. There is no right way to grieve. I counsel families to take their time, to be gentle and patient with themselves and with others. That's really all they can do.

Recently I was asked to sit with a man who, in the nurse's opinion, had only hours to live. When I got to his room, the first thing I noticed was the beautiful array of plants he had on his windowsill. He was semi-conscious, so I went over to look at his plants and then came to his bedside to announce my presence. "Paul," I said. "I'm here."

Paul opened his eyes, looked at me and smiled. He said, "Oh good. You're here. Will you take care of my plants for me?"

"Of course I will."

Paul smiled again, sighed and said, "Oh, good." That was it. He was gone.

Valentine's Day
1965

BY
BARBARA YOUNGER

Do you have one? A Valentine's Day gone wrong? I did. 1965. The Fifth Grade Valentine's Day Square Dance. Hampton Elementary School. Towson, Maryland.

At the practice dance the day before, one of the cool, cute boys asked me to be his partner. Yes! I was set for the real shindig. I was sure of it. We would dance together again on February 14. On Valentine's morning, the boys began inviting girls to be their partners. (No, we girls didn't ask the boys in 1965.) The oh-so-cute, cool boy asked another girl. Devastation for this 11-year-old. Soon almost everyone was paired up. Poor Barbara. No one to do-si-do with.

Finally, one of my friends did some negotiating, and Eddie Pissaro asked me to be his dance partner. Not anywhere near my first choice. I still remember how lumpy and sweaty his arm felt as we promenaded right and left.

FAST FORWARD 45 YEARS to my dad's memorial service.

"Barbara, I'm Eddie Pissaro."

The name shot through me like an arrow from a winged cherub.

"Eddie! How wonderful to see you! You knew my father?"

"I live in your old neighborhood now. When your dad was out raking leaves, I'd stop and chat with him."

We reminisced a bit about Hampton Elementary School and the kids we knew there.

And now, *ta da*! I would make his day. (My girls had told me that despite my lack of eye makeup, I looked pretty good in my funeral dress.)

"I haven't forgotten you were my partner for the Fifth Grade Square Dance."

"I was?" said Eddie. "I don't remember."

"You don't?"

Eddie shook his head. "No."

How could he forget?

THAT WEEK, when I came home to Hillsborough, I did a bit of archival research in my closet. I found a photo of me aged about 11: A goofy-looking girl with glasses in a bright pink velvet jumper. Wasn't I the dream date!

"Your dad was a good guy," Eddie said as he left the church that August day.

"Thanks, Eddie."

I should have added, "You're a good guy too, and on February 14, 1965, you were a *really* good guy. What an honor to be your square dance partner."

Serene Green

BY
JUDY ACKLEY BROWN

"In every walk of nature,
one receives more than he seeks."
John Muir

TURN GREEN! Not green with envy. Nor the yucky sick green. But relish the color green, all around you.

As I drove to my mother's house the other day, I took note of how lush and green the surroundings were and how subtle its effects are.

There is a new type of therapy called Green Therapy or Eco Therapy. The Japanese call it *Shinrin-yoku* or forest bathing. Even the name "forest bathing" sounds soothing.

Green Therapy is said to help children with ADHD, reduce stress and pain, increase immunity, and even help nursing home patients who suffer from dementia type anxiety.

I find this concept ironic but affirming. It is so basic. Our ancestral hunter-gatherer relatives are probably shaking their heads in disbelief. Fresh air and absorbing nature is now a therapy!

Green is my favorite color. My house is green, my upstairs is painted green, my bedspread is a green floral print, and my dining room lamp has a green patina. When we built our house many years ago our lighting salesman told me I was "greening out".

Feng shui wise, the color green is said to have a calming and restful effect. It creates balance and harmony. Some say it is the color of intimacy.

The crisp air of fall is arriving soon and the colors will change from green to oranges and reds and browns.

Whatever your source may be, whether it is sitting under a wispy willow or on blades of bluegrass, in your flower garden or the deep woods, watching a caterpillar or listening to the sounds of crickets and frogs, even eating spinach or sipping green tea; take in some green!

Take a bath in the forest!

The Sea As Smooth As Glass

BY
DONNA K. BARRY

"The sea is as smooth as glass. Let's take off our
shoes
and stockings, and paddle."
The Pirates of Penzance, Gilbert and Sullivan

THE TWO STRETCHED OUT on the sandy beach,
tired from clambering across the rocky shore.
Done with wading through water waist deep, done
with searching through wave-washed stones. The
heat beat up from the 100-degree sand.

"It's too hot and too bright to read," she said.

"It's too hot to walk anymore," he said.

The two sat in companionable silence, appreciating every small whiff of breeze coming off the water.

"What can we do?" she said. "We never relax," he said. "We're always doing something."

"It's true," she said. "Even when we think we're relaxing, we're not. We pop up from watching TV to do ironing or dishes. We never sit still. We're too busy seizing life, afraid to miss something and grow old."

"Why don't we just relax?" he said. "We hardly ever do."

And so the two sat stretched out upon the sultry beach. They watched the distant storm clouds gather. They watched birds glide overhead. They savored the increasing wisps of breezes. And they relaxed.

Contributors

DONNA K. BARRY is a nurse practitioner and blogs at **http://huffygirl.wordpress.com** where she writes about family, health and exercise, offers some satirical hyperbole, and rants against the overuse of cheese in the American diet. She is an avid cyclist, gardener and amateur photographer, featuring many of her cycling exploits and nature photographs on her blog. Donna is a graduate of Butterworth Hospital School of Nursing, and holds a Bachelor of Science in nursing from Western Michigan University and a Master of Science in nursing from the University of Michigan. Her clinical interests include encouraging patients to be partners in their health care and providing education for managing chronic illness and disease prevention. She has two grown sons, and lives with her husband in Michigan.

JUDY ACKLEY BROWN lives in Hillsborough, North Carolina, with her husband, Martin. She grew up in Rio de Janeiro, Brazil, and graduated from Connecticut College with a Bachelor of Arts degree in Biology, giving her a lifelong interest in alternative medicine and nutrition.

Judy works as an administrative assistant at New Hope Camp and Conference Center, a Presbyterian retreat center. She loves to travel and explore and take photographs. She's a hiker and loves to read. Judy and Martin have two grown children, a daughter, Jamie, who lives in New York City and a son, Tyler, who is attends law school in Washington DC.

STACEY E. CARON is an antiques dealer and art appraiser and owns her own business in New Jersey. She cooks as a hobby and entertains as much as possible! Al fresco dining is her favorite way to eat, and summer is her favorite season because of all the beautiful local produce. Stacey travels to New York City and Paris as much as she can to sample all the great food. She uses other people's recipes, as well as her own, and is addicted to making savory tarts. Her blog is **www.staceysnacksonline.com**.

BARBARA CHAPMAN and her husband, Bill, live in coastal Connecticut where they raised their two sons and a daughter. They now tend to the needs of their Basset Hound, Quinn. An 11-year survivor of breast cancer and having lived with multiple sclerosis for 20 years, Barbara works for Hospice of Middlesex County, Connecticut, in patient care liaison, helping terminally ill patients and their families. She taught pre-school for many years, and enjoys writing, reading, and being treated to lunch.

GABI COATSWORTH is a British-born writer who has spent half her life in the United States. She has been writing fiction for the past 10 years and has had work published in *Perspectives*, a Connecticut literary journal, and the *Rio Grande Review* (University of Texas at El Paso). Her story, *Farewell, Finally*, won first place in the *Connecticut Muse* Winter Essay Contest 2008. She won the Fairfield Arts Council Poetry Contest 2009, with her poem *To My Sister*, which has also been published online (TheSisterProject.com) and in this anthology. *Mused*, an online and print magazine, published her story, *Kitten con Brio*, in 2011. She writes a blog for writers (WriteConnexion.wordpress.com) as well as a personal blog, **www.gabicoatsworth.com**.

She lives in Connecticut and New Hampshire, with her husband.

Dawn Quyle Landau was raised in the coastal town of Scituate, Massachusetts. She attended Lesley College in Cambridge, Massachusetts, and graduate school in Hartford, Connecticut, receiving an MSW in 1985. After 13 years in the Midwest, she and her family moved to the Pacific Northwest in 2001. The San Juan Islands and Puget Sound inspire her daily. She loves hiking, skiing, cycling, sailing, drawing and enjoying all that the area has to offer.

Married for more than 25 years, and with three children, Dawn has been writing all her life. She won a "Pulitzer" in the 6th grade for a short story. Her travel and food reviews appear in *Cascadia Weekly* and she has a novel in progress. She started her blog **talesfromthemotherland.me** in July 2011 to express herself on the many aspects of being a mother, wife and woman.

Chris Rosen divides her time between her newly adopted home in Charlottesville, Virginia, and

Nashville, Tennessee. She first started writing for *The Berkshire Eagle* and found the discipline of a newspaper deadline, and working at home, fit into her family life.

After a move back to her home state of New Jersey, Rosen was given her own column at *The Two River Times*, where she blended local and political issues with personal reflections. She is married to Bob, an ER doctor, and they have two adult children and a son-in-law. In her blog, **mountainmornings. wordpress.com**, Chris refers to her daughter, an ER doctor, as The Bride, and her son-in-law, also a physician, as The Groom. Her son, The Rocker, is a guitarist with his band, The Parlor Mob.

LEAH R. SINGER is a writer and the owner of What's Your Story? providing writing and marketing strategy to small businesses, entrepreneurs, non-profits, and educational institutions. Leah also writes regularly for *The Huffington Post, Millionaire Girls Movement, Red Tricycle, Interfaith Family, Edible San Diego, Natural Kidz* and *360* magazine and other national blogs and websites. She blogs at **www.leahsthoughts. com** where she shares her stories of motherhood, cooking, photography, and whatever else comes to mind. Leah lives in San Diego, California, with her husband and daughter.

MADELINE G. TAYLOR lives in Silver Spring, Maryland, with her husband, daughter, cat and dog. She is an elementary ESOL teacher and loves what she does. Besides spending time with her family and teaching, Madeline is a baker, reader and craft-hobbyist. She likes to swim, bike and run, and occasionally does all three in one day.

PATTI WINKER created www.RemarkableWrinklies.com. Happily married with a big family and great-grandkids, she does ghostwriting, and published an ecookbook (www.MemoryLaneMeals.com). She writes about her experiences growing up in the 1950s and 1960s in a family of 11 children and loves to ride her bike. When Patti turned 50, she started walking marathons. She's walked three . . . so far.

LISA K. WINKLER is the author of *On the Trail of the Ancestors: A Black Cowboy's Ride Across America*. She worked as a reporter at the *Danbury*

News-Times, Connecticut, before becoming a teacher, and writes for professional journals, *Education Update*, *JerseyMan*, and study guides for Penguin Books.

Lisa wrote "The Kentucky Derby's Forgotten Jockeys" for *Smithsonian* magazine's website, www.smithsonian.com. (April, 2009). Two essays have been published in book anthologies, one for *Wisdom of Our Mothers* (Familia Books) and the other in *College Search and Parent Rescue: Essays for Parents by Parents of College-Going Students* (St. Martin's Press).

She taught middle school Language Arts for more than 15 years and served as a literacy consultant in Newark, New Jersey. She lives in Summit, New Jersey, and has three children and three grandchildren. She loves cycling, knitting, yoga, cooking, travel, theater and museums. Lisa is the founder of Chestnut Hill Press, which published *Tangerine Tango: Women Writers Share Slices of Life*. Her website is **www.lisakwinkler.com**.

BARBARA YOUNGER created **www.FriendfortheRide. com**, the blog where she provides encouraging words for the "Menopause Roller Coaster". With an MFA in Writing from Vermont College of Fine Arts, Barbara is the author of 21 books for adults and children (**BarbaraKYounger.com**). Her picture book, *Purple Mountain Majesties: The Story of Katharine Lee Bates and "America the Beautiful"*, received a starred review in Kirkus and was a Junior Library Guild Selection.

Barbara majored in French literature and history at Duke University and then earned a Master of Library Science from the University of North Carolina at Chapel Hill. She worked first as a school librarian and then a children's librarian in a public library.

Along with her writing, Barbara tutors student writers at Piedmont Community College and critiques picture-book and middle-grade novel manuscripts. She lives in a 180-year-old house in Hillsborough, North Carolina, with her husband Cliff and collections of everything from buttons to dolls to butter boxes. She's the mother of two grown daughters and is delighted to be grandmother to a baby boy.

Proceeds from the sale of the book will be given to charity. Follow our blogs for future notices.

Made in the USA
Charleston, SC
19 March 2016